AT THE EDGE OF HOPE

The Arthur Vining Davis Foundations are providing
copies of At the Edge of Hope *for professors and students*
in theological seminary communities and
for religious educators.

Lincoln Christian College

WITH CONTRIBUTIONS BY:
Peter L. Berger
Peter F. Drucker
Gerald R. Ford
Thomas E. Howard
Eugene C. Kennedy
Festo Kivengere
Martin E. Marty
Abigail McCarthy
Malcolm Muggeridge
John P. Newport
Armand M. Nicholi
Michael Novak
Thomas M. Reavley
James Reston

AT THE EDGE OF HOPE
OF HOPE
CHRISTIAN LAITY IN PARADOX

by Howard Butt
with Elliott Wright

A CROSSROAD BOOK · THE SEABURY PRESS · NEW YORK

1978
The Seabury Press
815 Second Avenue
New York, N.Y. 10017

Library of Congress Cataloging in Publication Data
North American Congress of the Laity, Los Angeles 1978.
At the edge of hope.
1. Laity—Congresses.   2. Civilization, Modern—1950–
—Congresses.   3. Social ethics—Congresses.   I. Butt, Howard.
II. Wright, H. Elliott, 1937–   III. Title.
BV687.N67 1978   262′.15   78-11729
ISBN: 0-8164-0414-3
ISBN: 0-8164-2614-7 Pbk.

CONTENTS

Part III:
PARADOXICAL HOPE

OVERVIEW

Conclusion:
BEING WITNESSES

THE INCANDESCENT PARADOX

The North American Congress of the Laity ended at noon-time on a bright California Monday with a mind-stretching, soul-stirring exchange on Christian hope and despair.

Malcolm Muggeridge, surveying our world as only a writer of his scope and brilliance can, had just announced the futility of all human systems, institutions, and proposed panaceas for our problems. In his speech, the British social wit, as famous these days for his rediscovery of Jesus as for crusty criticism, disposed of the allurements of both the Soviet Union and the United States, contemporary rival models for "a man-made kingdom of heaven on earth." Each, he said, promises freedom, prosperity, and peace, and both fail to deliver. Power and privation, according to Muggeridge, are the real foundations of the Soviet utopian prospectus; affluence and self-indulgence the spoilers of the American, symbol to him of hopelessly decayed Western civilization: "Food, drugs, beauty, and gas—the four pillars of the American way of life," he said.

Despairing of any earthly law, political structure, or human ideology as a source of freedom and the good life, Muggeridge proposed a more spiritual, a transcendent, agenda for hope and Christian awareness. Concentrate, he advised, on the "wonders of God's love flooding the universe" and touching personal lives.

Muggeridge had concluded with a rousing affirmation of personal faith in the God who frees him from the "dungeon of ego"; then, as the program called for, he sat down to discuss what he had said with a panel of notable American lay Christians.

Peter Berger, the distinguished sociologist, rose to Muggeridge's otherworldliness with another understanding of Christian hope: "Compared to the freedom which is promised to us in the Gospel, of course, all the utopias of this world, in fact, all of the realities of this world, are shabby and imperfect, and this we have to believe as Christians. I completely agree with everything you said about that. But . . ."

But what about Christian hope as an immanent operating force in the world? What about Christians as people of hope in everyday affairs? The Rutgers University professor, a Lutheran well known for work in the sociology of religion, was fearful that dismissal of the differences between competing political systems denigrates Christian moral responsibility in the social realm. Berger doubted the helpfulness of saying it makes no difference what happens to the U.S. and the U.S.S.R., the two major utopian models of our times. "There are enormous differences between the two and it's important for reasons of Christian ethics to emphasize those differences," he said, clearly preferring imperfect U.S. society to Soviet totalitarianism. Berger continued, "Now . . . I'm not at all suggesting that America is perfect, that we should strut around in some sort of happy self-righteousness. We have done terrible things in our society and we still have an agenda of rights and wrongs which is far from finished . . . , but I think we have enormous resources of decency, of goodwill, and we have institutions which can translate decency into political hope."

Is this world, imperfect as it is, nothing but "a night in which all cats are gray?" Berger said Christians can afford a more hopeful approach to solving problems and correcting wrongs.

The congress audience, almost eight hundred of us gathered in Los Angeles, leaned forward into the debate. All of us, Protestant and Roman Catholic; U.S. citizen; Canadian or Mexican; men and women; black and white; instinctively knew the issue of Christian hope in a sinful world is of first magnitude for believers in any generation. It was a fitting climax to our four days, February 17–20, 1978, spent exploring the theme, "Divine Creation: Human Creativity."

Muggeridge agreed in part with Berger, disagreed on the whole. Has Western civilization, despite its dependence on Christian metaphors of reality, passed the point of no return? For the sake of his grandchildren, Muggeridge hoped he was wrong: "I personally think it has"—too much self-indulgence in materialism, pornography, Muzak, "Newzak," and motorcars.

No, the Christian Gospel is not without power for social therapy, even today. Another voice joined the gripping exchange. Michael Novak, the columnist and Roman Catholic theologian, also a panel member, was unhappy with Muggeridge's suggestion that a Christian's involvement in politics is comparable to a pianist in a brothel occasionally playing "Abide with Me" to elevate his surroundings. Is Christian hope only private? Has it no social expressions? Can a civilization not be "born again"?

"Of course, civilizations die," said Novak. "A lot of them have died and this one will die and yet the Lord incarnates himself in one after the other; gives us signs in one after the other, and out of the ashes of this one yet another will be born until the trumpet blast will release us, but we must struggle (in the world) until that trumpet."

A second wind might be possible for a civilization, Muggeridge granted, not "born again in eternity." Everything but the eternal is paltry, he said.

Paltry, imperfect but hardly expendable, Berger replied. "What does it mean for a Christian to be *in the world*? That, it seems to me, is what this congress is all about—the laity in the world. People are not professionally concerned with religion but concerned with other things. While we have been talking about civilization and politics and America, we could talk about worldly problems people have in their personal lives, whether it's with illness, or children, or frustrations at work. And I think there are always two things one can say as a Christian about worldly things. One is what Mr. Muggeridge said very eloquently and very correctly—that ". . . in the end none of it matters. But on the other hand, until the end, it matters a good deal."

In the meantime, until the final trumpet, as Novak said, Berger found it necessary for Christians to draw connections between the private and the political, "Any act to produce more justice is tainted. . . . It often leads to consequences unforeseen and the opposite of what anyone hoped for. Nevertheless, I think there are moments in history when certain actions in the name of justice point to God's justice and, by that token, are lifted above the misery of this world. . . . Now, I think the same can be said of personal life: Tainted human acts can point to God's love."

"I like that very much," said Muggeridge, revising somewhat earlier remarks about the blessedness of material poverty. But the British journalist finally held to his claim that the only important reality is personal experience of the light of God's love brought into the dimension of time.

Electric tension rippled through the congress. Part of the crowd applauded Muggeridge. Part applauded Berger.

I applauded them both.

The *Times* of London, reporting the exchange, said the Congress of the Laity ended on a note of controversy. I saw it, rather, as a moment of incandescent paradox, profound as the Gospel itself, a door to peacemaking, a prelude to the reconciliation of long-opposing theological views. What enthralled me as I listened was not a duel between hope and despair. What came to light was a paradox within hope itself. The apparent contradictions of hope "out of" and "in" this world were actually complementary. Muggeridge's transcendent hope and Berger's immanent hope are both essential parts of the Christian message, both are true, each needs the other. Hope transcendent and hope immanent must cohere, even as they contend, in order to intersect and overcome despair—the loss of expectation, both expectation for God's eternal Kingdom and expectation for the improvement of this world.

The paradox of other-worldly and this-worldly hope as it contradicts despair, as it elevates expectation, offers light to Christians as we seek to experience and express faith today and to cope in redemptive ways with the personal, cultural, and political problems plaguing us. Paradox is not usually thought of as "incandescent," as illuminating, yet in this case the description is apt. Our pathway is brightened by the realization that Muggeridge's transcendent expectation and Berger's immanent expectation form one complete Christian hope. The first says, turn to God because the human prospect is so bleak; the second says, the human prospect can be changed because of God. Grasping the interpenetration of these apparently opposite theological perspectives helps us to keep transcendence and immanence together, as they unequivocally are in Jesus Christ—divine and human.

My topic in this book is the Christian laity of North America as a dynamic force for Christ and the church in the late twentieth century, and the logical place to begin, it seems to me, is with paradoxical hope as it intersects despair. To raise the issues of lay witness and service is to introduce tensions having to do with "the other world" and "this world" and also, on the level of experience, tensions between pessimism and optimism about this world.

A battery of voices come at the modern laity: "Win souls . . . feed the hungry . . . praise God . . . fight human oppression . . . deepen spiritual life . . . renew the church . . . build a better society." These voices come from preachers, bishops, denominational assemblies, lay organizations, and all manner of individuals, believers and unbelievers, who expect something of the *laos*—the people of God. And these calls, demands, and proposals reflect presuppositions about the nature of hope. Conservative Christians, evangelicals and others, who emphasize soul-winning—personal conversion—have a way of neglecting the Christian responsibility in society. Their stress on transcendence invites reminder that Christians believe God entered the world in the earthly form of Jesus, who established an immanent body, the church. The Incarnation itself gives good reason to expect signs of the wondrous love of God in human ventures. Liberal Christians, who often concentrate on lay obligation in social causes, project an optimism about human ability and goodness that history so far fails to support. Their focus on the immanent needs reminder that people are never the designers of the eternal Kingdom we Christians expect.

Conservative "otherworldly" hope and liberal "this worldly" hope are dangled like competing pearls of great price before the laity today. What tragedy, when they really form a single unified reality. Transcendence and immanence as they affect Christian discipleship are inseparably linked, and that is the first thing to say in any book on the laity as a dynamic force for Christ and the church. Everything is hopeless but God. Everything is hopeful because of God.

Hope with its paradox intersects despair, elevates expectation, but we must honestly acknowledge that hope and despair, optimism and pessimism, mingle in the everyday experiences and emotions of the laity and, thereby, influence attitudes toward witness and service. Today, we believe everything will work out for the best: the brother-in-law will get a job, prices will go down, our congregation will hold together in the squabble over the pastor, the next mayor will clean up city hall, and God will somehow, and soon, put an end to evil; then tomorrow, we are hopeless about everything except, perhaps, a small warm feeling inside, which we identify with a God we believe must be out there and who visits individual hearts.

The world we see and know day-to-day—the setting for lay witness and service—is a place of considerable darkness, as Michael Novak pointed out in a discussion at the Congress of the Laity. Christians respond in faith to the light of God's wondrous love, yet perceive that light through St. Paul's "glass darkly." It is a world of shadows, half-formed images, tensions and uncertainties, in which the laity exists, hoping and despairing in God.

To put it another way: Christians live at the edge of hope. Any edge can be viewed from two perspectives. Move a pencil across a common sheet of paper and it soon goes off the edge. But slide the pencil along a desk top toward the paper and it hits the edge. Is the edge where the paper stops or starts? Both, obviously, and so it is with the edge of hope, where confidence and doubt resound with the rhythms of heaven and hell.

At the edge of hope, Christians are part of God's lovingly created, tragically fallen world; we are imbued with vision of a better order, a fully redeemed creation, a heavenly city, but wonder how, or if, the vision relates to history, to time, and to eternity. At the edge of hope, the outline of glory and the framework of chaos collide. Knowing that we and our societies are nothing compared with God, but confident that we and our world are beloved of God, the laity makes pilgrimage and finds vocation.

A very helpful book would describe individual lay persons and groups of laity currently making their Christian pilgrimage and finding Christian vocation. All too little journalism is devoted to the specifics of modern lay ministry and mission. Another book could supplement those already numerous on methods for enlivening and channeling lay commitment. This is neither of those books, although examples of various lay responses to the Lord and some of the proposals for broadening the lay awakening are mentioned. Nor is this a militant defense of lay rights in the churches, though the rights and responsibilities of laity in organized Christianity are asserted.

The laity as a dynamic force for Christ involves more than methodology, more than an end to ecclesiastical discrimination against lay men and women. As important as those issues, and as foundation for them, is the role of the laity in grappling with the array of personal, theological, cultural, and social issues joined at what I am calling the edge of hope.

This book is, in a sense, itself a paradox: less about the mechanics of lay witness and service than about a creative, responsive lay mind-set needed as leaven in church and society; more about breaking through denominational, theological, and political barriers than about breaking down ecclesiastical doors.

North America's Christian laity is alive, vigorous in witnessing to the transforming power of faith in Christ, and increasingly able to bring enormous intellectual resources to bear on theological and social issues. I am especially concerned in this book to point to and encourage lay intellectual prowess as it can contribute to theological reflection and social improvement in this imperfect world where Christians await their Lord. The laity has a ministry of mind as well as ministries of heart and hand, and we need all the minds we can get working together at the edge of hope.

The contents are drawn in large part from the earlier-mentioned Congress of the Laity, held February 17–20, 1978, in Los Angeles. Careful attention should be given to the phrase "*of* the laity"—not *on* the laity. Our gathering was only mildly seasoned with such questions as: What is the laity? How does it function? And how does it relate to the ordained ministry?—questions often of more formal interest to the clergy than to the laity itself. We issued no proclamations about or to the laity. Rather, the congress was a voluntary assembly of denominationally, racially, and culturally diverse Christians, the great majority of whom were of the laity, come together in response to a specific invitation. Since the congress and this book serve similar purposes, it is in order—indeed, necessary—to describe briefly how the Congress of the Laity came about, what it was, and, then, to explain how material from it is used throughout the book.

Issued in the autumn of 1977, the congress proclamation and invitation said:

> The contemporary world cries out for creative, moral leadership. In response, we are calling together men and women of prominence and influence—from government and business, from science and the arts, from the professions, from sports and entertainment and from family life—who are open to the leadership of Jesus Christ.
>
> Together we will break through the traditional barriers between liberals and conservatives, strengthen the best in both, calling each of us to creative change. We will examine the tensions between secular leadership and Christian discipleship, explore the interactions between Christianity and our culture, discover the intellectual, psychological and artistic implications of faith, and build bridges of mutual support.

The degree to which the four-day agenda fostered the noble intentions of lowering barriers and building bridges is something those in attendance are deciding in their own lives. Immediate and continuing participant responses have indicated at least a strong agreement with the proposition that Christians should reach over and through such traditional dividers as denomination, race, nationality, and social status. And the congress program provided an abundance of serious, exciting exploration of tensions and interactions between Christianity and secular culture, and a superabundance of intellectual challenge. The exploration and the intellectual challenge, as reflected in a variety of congress segments, are the grist in the ensuing chapters.

The proclamation was made over my signature as general chairman but I hardly acted alone. Behind the congress was the long-standing commitment of the H. E. Butt Foundation, a family philanthropy, to the development of lay leadership and to lay theological education. Beside me were colleagues and friends, especially other staff members of the foundation and of two other family-related public charities, Christian Men, Inc., and the Laity Lodge Foundation. Foremost among those standing beside me was my wife, Barbara Dan Butt, a companion of remarkable Christian insight. Our small group, in consultation with associates across the country, shared and honed a perhaps audacious vision—the vision of three small Texas operations of evangelical Protestant reputation serving God by stepping onto the national stage with a message of Christian reconciliation, with a bid for greater lay involvement in intellectual and social discourse, and with a clarion call for Christians to hold to hope in the midst of a shabby, secular society.

Christian Men, Inc., took the responsibility for planning the Congress of the Laity. That organization, founded in 1960, embodies the lay ministry commitment of the Butt Foundation, established by my father and mother with resources earned primarily in the grocery business. In the nineteen sixties, Christian Men's Layman's Leadership Institutes for business and professional leaders became a model for many of the Christian lay seminars now held throughout the United States and Canada. Its program also includes lay renewal retreats at Laity Lodge, located at the H. E. Butt Foundation Camp in the Texas hill country west of San Antonio.

Through the foundation activities, lay evangelism, and our various ministries, I have been extremely close to the lay witness and lay leadership movements in that branch of American Prostestantism we call "evangelical."

The word "evangelical" comes from the New Testament term for "gospel" or "good news." In its German form, stemming from the sixteenth-century Reformation, it means simply "Protestant." In North America, "evangelical" is used in a variety of ways: sometimes and incorrectly, as a synonym for "biblical fundamentalist"; at other times to specify members of certain particularistic, theologically conservative denominations, and, most recently, as an umbrella for a great diversity of groups and sentiments that in some way make an appeal to orthodoxy. While no definition of the word will ever please everyone, the marks of the evangelical today are, generally, emphasis on the atonement, the death, and the resurrection of Jesus; reliance on the Bible as the sole source of Christian authority; and skepticism of liberal optimism about the perfectibility of human society. All evangelicals are not biblical literalists. All evangelicals do not reject liturgical worship or Christian social action, or turn their faces to the wall at the mention of the National Council of Churches. Almost all evangelicals do believe that personal experience of the dying-rising Christ is the beginning point of Christian discipleship.

I cherish and want to deepen my evangelical roots, but in my personal pilgrimage I discovered it is important to be a Christian first and an evangelical second. I thank God I learned to distrust the treacherous currents of religious party spirit and to increasingly trust the Lord who turned me toward the larger Christian community. I grew impatient over the years with labels and innuendos from any side that hamper an expanding life of love in Christ.

As my own evangelical education was proceeding, fresh winds were blowing through the larger Christian community in North America. A desire for Christian unity was spreading—a desire manifested less in plans for church union than in the erosion of hostilities among the members of historically divided churches. Catholics and Protestants were getting to know one another not as stereotypes but as disciples of the Lord. The laity was growing more assertive, and in the midnineteen seventies the press announced a new evangelical revival.

A renewed American interest in religion seemed to be a social fact by the year of the United States Bicentennial. Celebration of the secular was being replaced by quests for the sacred. I felt encouraged, though hardly pleased, by all the indicators of an upsurge in religious enthusiasm. As a Christian, I did not applaud (although I might understand) the proliferation of bizarre sects and eclectic cults competing for the favors of the young, and I held an abiding abhorrence of peddling the human potential movement as adequate or ultimate faith. But I was inspired and excited over the new and deepening personal commitment among thousands of salt-of-the-earth lay Christians.

Overjoyed as I was, I had (and have) some concerns about the much—likely, too much—publicized "evangelical awakening." What direction was the revival taking? Would it veer into cultural deadends (as some say both old-style religious conservatism and liberalism have) or would it creatively engage the broad currents of contemporary history? Could personal Christianity become a force of social renewal and overcome divisions which weaken Christian witness?

Another question: Could small, stumbling Christian service organizations based in Texas help to raise the issues that, if dealt with, would contribute to the maturity of the new awakening? Any religious revival is short-lived if it does not move beyond the first flush to a maturing appreciation of the implications of faith. Would the new awakening be like the teen-ager converted at a June tent-meeting, who carried the Bible constantly until the Fourth of July picnic when the Holy Writ was left by the swimming pool, never to be reclaimed? Or could it, like the first and second "Great Awakenings" of the American past, mature and make a social difference?

One of my strongest convictions is that the North American Christian laity, men and women, individually and corporately, are the most potentially potent force we have for evangelism and for socioeconomic justice, political morality, and cultural integrity. That potential cannot be realized, however, if, in a modern version of the Corinthians' bickering over who converted whom, we continue to divide ourselves: "My faith is personal. . . . My faith is public. . . . I win souls. . . . I do social action. . . . I'm a Baptist. . . . I'm Catholic. . . . I take Holy Communion sitting down. . . . I commune on my knees." No! The Lord prayed that we shall all be one, and so we are whether we like it or not, if we love God and one another.

Our little group in Texas talked, prayed, pondered, prayed some more, and decided to call a Congress of the Laity.

Two years before the congress convened, the small staffs of Christian Men, Inc., Laity Lodge Foundation, and the Butt Foundation went to work on the dream. Along the way we were also taking other initiatives to foster the vision of Christian reconciliation and lay involvement in social discourse. For example, Christian Men, Inc., joined with the Council of Southwestern Theological Schools, composed of eleven Protestant and Catholic institutions, in sponsoring community-based seminars in lay theological education. Laity Lodge's programs became more broadly ecumenical, and on October 12–15, 1977, the lodge was the site of a meeting of the National Council of Churches' Commission on Faith and Order, made up of Protestant, Catholic, and Eastern Orthodox representatives.

The details of planning a congress for which there was no direct precedent are interesting but need not be outlined here. It is important to set forth the three issues uppermost in our minds as the planning proceeded. These issues have been mentioned earlier in passing, but each should be stated more fully. They are Christian unity, lay intellectual maturity, and the interaction of Christianity and culture, notably, Christianity and culture in America.

1. Unity

Obviously, our concern for unity was not that of improving formal relations among church structures. Channels for that dimension of ecumenicity already exist and are the responsibility of the churches themselves. We were not interested in a conference of delegates—so many Episcopalians, so many Roman Catholics, so many Pentecostals. Our aim was to convene laity from all churches and theological persuasions who wanted to come together, in the phrase of Arthur C. McGill of Harvard Divinity School, "to look beyond traditional doctrines and familiar piety."

We were gladly aware that we were not lone pioneers in recognizing the value to Christianity of recruiting the laity to the work of healing rifts in the body of Christ. "People are not as far apart as labels have indicated," Lewis Smedes of Fuller Theological Seminary told a reporter at the congress. We wanted to dramatize that fact, and also a point succinctly put by William P. Thompson in the course of an interview during the meeting. "By and large, the laity is more inclined to reach out across denominational lines than are some of the clergy," said Thompson, a layman who is Stated Clerk of the United Presbyterian Church. We were motivated in no small part by an awareness that Christian reconciliation involves overcoming estrangements between clergy and laity.

Our particular angle on unity was in some measure a reflection of what Martin Marty, the perceptive church historian, sees as a contemporary attempt to "repeal" events that deeply divided the American Protestant community in the late nineteenth and early twentieth centuries. Offering a brief history lesson in a congress press conference, Marty explained that in the mid-to-late eighteeen hundreds, the United States Protestant family was fairly unified in its concentration on evangelism and on programs to improve society. Lay initiative was pivotal, as exemplified by Dwight L. Moody, evangelist, educator, and social therapist. Several developments, Marty said, resulted in party splits. One was the professionalization of ministry and church leadership, with the result that the role of the laity was depreciated. Another was the "modernist-fundamentalist" debate on the interpretation of Scripture. As a striking symbol of the rift between those who stressed personal evangelism and those concerned with social amelioration, Marty cited the omission of a department of evangelism when the Federal Council of Churches was created in 1908. Such a department was added later but the damage was done. Evangelicals tended

[15]

to steer clear of the council, that era's major ecumenical framework, which they considered in the hands of dangerous "liberals."

Happily, efforts to "repeal" the causes of Protestant party splits, including the estrangement of clergy and laity, coincides today with an unfolding ecumenical spirit and lay renewal movement in Catholicism. At least as it involves witness to Christ in the struggles of society, the overdue Christian family reunion can begin to look for the biggest meadow it can find.

2. Lay Intellectual Maturity

Two aspects of the much-discusssed contemporary "intellectual crisis" concerned us. First, evangelical antiintellectuality and, second, secular antifaith. Could the evangelical awakening possibly be fulfilled without producing more thoughtful expressions through which to engage the world? Is the intellectual arena by definition "secular"? Is authentic Christianity inevitably contemplative? Or is the "secular" need precisely for creative Christian thinking?

I was asked in Los Angeles if I think evangelicals have an "intellectual inferiority complex." I answered honestly, "Yes," and so I do believe, but as I reflect on the matter I am not convinced that the liberal or mainline Protestants or the Roman Catholics have any greater percentage of lay persons who use their intellect to full capacity as Christians. To have an intellectual inferiority complex is not to have an inferior intellect. Michael Novak made a telling observation in a congress session, which can be adapted to my point. He noted that many evangelicals and Catholics, once among the poorest and least-educated people in society, now have the affluence, the education, and the leisure to take their places in the leadership of government, the professions, science, and the arts. The intellectual capacity of the laity as a whole in North America is staggering.

Persons who call themselves Christians on Sunday, persons who may be "born again," persons who may thrill to the liturgy, or persons who always pay their parish pledge—these people demonstrate the intellectual and organizational capacity to run corporations and universities, build computers, cure disease, design skyscrapers, write books, and, in all kinds of jobs, keep the wheels of commerce and industry turning. But far, far too much of the intellectual power of the laity stays isolated in the secular arena, as though faith made no contact with reason or science or economics or all the other professions and the human relationships they entail. Is the intellect only secular unless it happens to belong to a preacher, priest, or seminary professor? I ask especially, can personal evangelical faith not be given social application, translated into the fearless judgment of modern-day Amoses responding to the cries of the hungry, the plight of the oppressed, tottering public morality, and public corruption? Can the church at its full potential, with its laity unleashed, motivated, and educated, not change society to degrees never yet imagined?

Can we not love God with active minds?

"This congress calls you to think from the lay position where you are six days per week," said Dorothy Height, president of the National Association of Negro Women. That was what we hoped to do and Miss Height's comment was most appreciated since she is a woman well known for thoughtful witness and service seven days per week the year round.

3. Interaction with Culture

Our third concern was intricately related to the second. We wanted to put together a congress that would encourage participants to deal with the possibility that the travail of Western civilization is essentially religious, and only secondarily political or economic. Never did we, as the *Times* of London mistakenly said of the congress, envision one common set of Christian values to which all Americans could subscribe. (As if without our individual emphases; as if without pluralistic differentiation.) Neither religion nor culture in Western civilization is monolithic—cannot and should not be monolithic.

Our interest in this area was in lay accountability for the condition of our culture as a whole, and in lay perception that no culture-bound Gospel (evangelical or liberal or whatever) offers hope or realistic alternatives for social change. With the latter in mind, we risked in our program content and organization the charge of being vague about what, if any, label went where, on whom, and on the congress itself. Any observer who described the meeting as an "evangelical rally" has never attended such a rally. As it turned out, fortunately, the congress had to be described on its own terms. Lewis Smedes of Fuller Seminary offered one of the most clever descriptions. He called it "a cocktail party" (although no cocktails were served) in the sense of T. S. Eliot's play *The Cocktail Party*. "Don't misunderstand," he said, "a cocktail party is where interesting people meet interesting people and act as catalysts on one another."

We selected as the theme the phrase, "Divine Creation: Human Creativity," a challenging combination of words with multiple meanings. "Divine Creation" calls to mind not only the beginning of the universe but also the continuing dynamic nature of God and, in some theological traditions, the re-creating act of God in Christ. "Human Creativity" is double-barreled in the context. It points to the responsibility assumed when persons respond to the good news that God is Love, meaning the creativity of believers should always be at the disposal of the Creator. At the same time, it recognizes that, no matter what one believes about God, people create; not *ex nihilo*, but out of the substance of this world people create societies, cultures, and languages; scientists organize the elements in new ways and turn docile atoms into bombs, and artists create music, poetry, drama, paintings, and sculpture. Implicit in the theme is the question, how do Christians interpret the creative energies of persons who have no apparent consciousness of or commitment to the Creator?

The emphasis on creativity naturally suggested the inclusion of the arts in the congress experience, as will be explained at a later point. One of my disappointments is that this book cannot adequately reflect the contributions of musicians, dancers, actors, painters, and photographers to the congress.

Our intention to explore the relationships between the

divine and the human, between faith and practice, Christianity and culture inspired the "creation" of several new terms for program ingredients. Bible study sessions were "theoquests." Workshops covering two dozen issues were "theoventures." Panel discussions following each of five keynote speakers were "theoprobes," and the artists-in-residence were part of the "theoform."

I am not sure I would want our "theo-" words to enter the current religious language, where any new term has a way of becoming jargon. They served well for one-time use. We were probing, questing, venturing, and dealing with art forms to better understand the divine Creator, and how our creativity relates to God's.

If we originally overestimated the number of United States senators, university presidents, and chairmen of *Fortune* five hundred companies "open to the leadership of Jesus Christ" through a lay congress, we did not underestimate general interest in our risky project. Former President and Mrs. Gerald Ford agreed to act as honorary chairpersons and were present at the opening session, despite Mrs. Ford's fragile health in February 1978. The convenors, who were mostly persons affiliated with Butt family charities, received valuable guidance from a panel of advisors whose members ranged from a Harvard psychiatrist in the East to a San Francisco book publisher in the West. The diversity of a larger group of inviters, persons asked to propose participants, can be shown by noting that alphabetically the list began with Steve Allen, the actor, and ended with Andrew Young, the United States ambassador to the United Nations.

Three theological seminaries in southern California cooperated splendidly as regional hosts. Those were Fuller Theological Seminary, a nondenominational institution of evangelical heritage at Pasadena; St. John's School of Theology, a Roman Catholic seminary at Camarillo; and Claremont School of Theology, which has affiliations with the United Methodist Church and the United Church of Christ.

Since foundation funds for the congress were restricted, a per person registration fee of two hundred dollars was necessary, although we were able to absorb the cost for a limited number of seminary students and others who served the congress in various capacities. The family charities contributed some three hundred fifty thousand dollars to the congress bill of approximately five hundred thousand dollars.

Total registration was 792 persons. Not everyone chose to list a denominational affiliation and none was required, but of those who filled in that blank, 239 were Presbyterians, 108 Methodists, 99 Baptists, 73 Roman Catholics, 62 Episcopalians, 30 Lutherans, 20 members of the United Church of Christ, and 72 affiliated with other churches. Participants from Canda numbered 34; from Mexico 30. About 150 persons came from United States ethnic minority groups.

We were, of course, criticized from several and sometimes opposing directions on the congress composition. Where are the poor? Where are the rich? Why no members of President Carter's cabinet? Why no more ethnic minorities? Why no discernible charismatic presence? Why no display for Athletes for Christ?

I expected such questions and feel not the least defensive when they are asked. Most of the criticisms were of the kind that volunteer-defender Martin Marty calls, "Where's Johnny's cap?" The familiar story comes from Winston Churchill. A man saves a drowning child and, when he delivers him home, the mother asks, "Where's Johnny's cap?"

Most of the participants were middle-echelon, middle-class Americans, including the ethnic minority men and women. Yet within that not inconsequential slice of the Christian community, the variety of theological, political, and cultural opinion was broad enough to evoke an unsolicited word of encouragement from Jorge Lara-Braud, the Mexican-American theologian in charge of the National Council of Churches' department of theological studies. "This is the most inclusive lay gathering I have ever attended," he said. "This congress has high potential for establishing a new and unprecedented coalition among Christians. We don't have a precedent for this, and it is no accident that it happened through the laity."

We started our initiative to promote Christian unity, lay intellectual maturity, and interaction between Christianity and culture where we, three small Texas charities, could start. I cannot believe God asks anything more, as long as we do not let the place where we start be the place we stop.

Selection of the congress leadership was a series of serendipities. We stoutly resisted the temptation to set up five ideological slots and then to recruit keynote speakers to fill them. Instead, we invited public figures and scholars who, we believed, could illumine the theme out of their own creative geniuses. We fared extremely well. Keynoters were Abigail McCarthy, novelist and Catholic lay leader; Peter Drucker, management consultant and author; James Reston, the Pulitzer Prize-winning New York *Times* columnist; John Newport, specialist in the arts and philosophy and professor at Rice University, Houston; and Malcolm Muggeridge.

To engage each keynote speaker in dialogue (theoprobe) after his or her address, we were fortunate to have Peter Berger and Michael Novak, identified earlier, and Thomas Howard, professor of English language and literature at Gordon College in Massachusetts—laymen all. Howard is an Episcopalian, an authority on C. S. Lewis, and a man whose evangelical bearing blends with admiration for the Anglo-Catholic reality. Gary Demarest, pastor of the La Canada Presbyterian Church, La Canada, California, and a congress convenor, served as moderator for the theoprobes.

We wanted Bible study in plenary sessions dealing with transcendence and immanence. Theoquesters were Martin Marty, a Lutheran, professor at the University of Chicago and associate editor of *The Christian Century;* Eugene Kennedy, a Roman Catholic professor of psychology at Loyola University, Chicago, and author of twenty-six books; and Bishop Festo Kivengere, exiled prelate of the Anglican Church of Uganda and modern evangelical saint.

The three parts of this book are built around the keynote addresses, the conversations following the speeches, the presentations of the Bible study leaders, and material gleaned from some of the twenty-four workshops. Additional information on the program participants and the relevance of their topics to the congress theme will be included at appropriate points in the ensuing chapters.

A mere collection of papers and proceedings from the Congress of the Laity did not seem in order because of the diffuse theme and the less-than-simple program design. Therefore, I have tried to originate a book format that will respect the freedom granted to the speakers and, at the same time, coherently present the contents and ethos of the Congress of the Laity to readers. The format, the framework I have chosen, is that of the paradox of hope wrestling with despair, the incandescent paradox emblazoned in my mind in the Berger-Muggeridge exchange already described. To me, the exchange crystalized the entire event.

Part I, "God, and the Ordinary," explores transcendent and immanent hope as it relates to creativity. Included are the presentations of Festo Kivengere, Eugene C. Kennedy, and Malcolm Muggeridge, plus a fuller elucidation of the exchange touched off by the British journalist.

Part II, "At the Edges in Life," investigates selected areas of human existence where Christians experience tensions, hopes, despairs, and seek to make a faithful witness to Christ. The five chapters deal specifically with lay responsibility, the arts and media, public life, organizations as modern realities, and the state of the family. Included are the addresses of Abigail McCarthy, John P. Newport, James Reston, and Peter Drucker. Some chapters, such as that on the family, rely heavily on congress workshops (theoventures).

Part III, "Paradoxical Hope," pinpoints the challenges to the creativity of contemporary lay Christians. Martin E. Marty's presentation and excerpts from a workshop led by the historian are included.

Formal papers are not necessarily used in the sequences in which they were given and, in some cases, have been edited for print. If a speaker was forced to cut a prepared text to keep within time limits, the longer version is used.

Before concluding this long introduction to a short book, I want to return to the other-worldly this-worldly paradox of hope intersecting despair. The exchange between Muggeridge and Berger crystalized the Congress of the Laity for me, but that does not mean the paradox was explicitly spelled out as I have put it. Following my own vision, I may be giving a quite personal cast to the congress. I think not, as I have reflected on the papers, reviewed the discussion, and listened to tapes of the workshops. At almost every point, I find transcendent and/or immanent hope wrestling with despair, as I shall try to point out in introducing and bridging the chapters.

As I understand the Christian faith, hope and despair themselves creatively interact even as they contradict. Hope can grow at the gnawing edges of despair; doubts about this world propel us toward God as center and source of confidence. With hope, transcendent and immanent, steadfast in God, we can take risks for the sake of love and justice in the imperfect here and now.

And frown or smile about the human condition, this much is sure: all of us live "in the meantime," "the until . . ."—until God fulfills the divine timetable; until God vindicates the processes begun in creation and in Christ, as theologian Richard John Neuhaus says. Until that day when God "will wipe away every tear" (Rev. 24:4), it is tempting to despair of all causes of tears, causes such as human relationships, and human institutions, and, because they go awry, human strategies for solving problems; we are tempted to despair of the tawdry, evil world and retreat into a private experience of God's love as though faith and hope were only for eternity and not also for time.

Further, since "the until . . ." seems so indefinite, so unscheduled by our clocks and calendars, we are likewise tempted to make ourselves God's supervisors; to substitute our temporal societies and civilizations, sometimes our denominations and lay organizations, for God's promised Kingdom. When this happens, when God's immanence is misidentified with ourselves and our creations, the reality of the everlasting transcending God is downplayed. In effect, we tell God to leave us to our own heavens, or hells. Adam and Eve hid from God among the trees of Eden; we try to hide in the forests of our earthly loves as though faith and hope were only for time and not also for eternity.

We live in "the until . . ." We expect another Kingdom, but in the meantime, until the consummation, this world is the only world we have. We—Christians—may not be *of* the world but we certainly are *in* it; and we are somehow unappreciative to God if we fail to care passionately about a world that, for better or worse, is home, if only temporarily. Dare we turn our backs on a world created in goodness, a very much fallen world, which the Gospel of John says Jesus Christ came not to condemn but to save? Care for the earth, God told Adam and Eve, and caring for earth includes caring for nature and people, societies and civilizations. Peace, justice, and feeding the hungry concerned Jesus Christ; so surely we who call ourselves Christians should be concerned.

At the same time, we dare not make an idol of the "here and now," as though our love and compassion for it are ends in themselves; as though our hope alone can save it.

Life at the edge of hope is, for a Christian, joyous, frightening, stimulating, bewildering, confident, despairing, and never, never dull; sometimes down but not out; rejoicing in all things—praising God from whom all blessings and challenges flow.

Part I

GOD, AND THE ORDINARY

He is the image of the invisible God, the first-born of all creation; for in him all things were created, in heaven and on earth, visible and invisible, whether thrones or dominions or principalities or authorities—all things were created through him and for him. He is before all things, and in him all things hold together. He is the head of the body, the church; he is the beginning, the first-born from the dead, that in everything he might be pre-eminent. For in him all the fulness of God was pleased to dwell, and through him to reconcile to himself all things, whether on earth or in heaven, making peace by the blood of his cross.

COLOSSIANS 1:15–20 (RSV)

OVERVIEW

We are on a "quest for meaning" today. All the psychologists, preachers, and newspaper columnists agree. Individuals and societies want something or somebody, an idea or experience, usually both, to answer the question asked of Alfie in the song popular a decade ago: "What's it all about?" We want to feel real, and for many that means becoming unreal by getting "high" on drugs, or on Jesus, or on anticipation—anticipation of Saturday night, the Olympic Games, or the next visit of the grandchildren. Some of us even want to feel useful: perhaps, to get "high" on a cause, be it peace or a renewed "cold war," ecology or an increase of the gross national product—some cause bigger than we are, a cause bestowing significance.

Failing to find anything external to "turn us on," we retreat into the personal self. It is no surprise that our list of best-selling books in the late nineteen seventies are dominated by thin, expensive volumes on physical and psychological self-impovement. Developing a slim, trim, runner's body, "looking good," or reordering our emotional furniture have taken on near-divine significance. And if our newly designed face or brain does not bring the meaning—the reality—we want, we can try Scope in the morning.

Our contemporary "quest for meaning" has a familiar echo. A generation ago we were told about the agonizing experience of "nothingness," a reverse way of saying people were looking for something, and back then almost every seminarian entertained, often mystified, adoring hometown congregations with sermons based on Jean-Paul Sartre's *No Exit* or T. S. Eliot's *The Waste Land*. We were mystified because in contrast to "nothing" we were experiencing so much, at least in America, which is the culture I mean.

In the immediate post–World War II era, our world was being changed by "cold war" politics; by intensified urbanization and racial tensions; by the original "rock 'n' roll" music; and by plastic, television, air travel, and other scientific marvels whose production had been escalated by military needs. Anyone who lived through the nineteen fifties knows that the period was not so drearily complacent, so uneventful as it seemed to the counter-culture gurus of the nineteen sixties. If we were experiencing the acute despair of "nothingness," we did not know it, but we had a sense that Marc Connelly's character in *Green Pastures* was describing our world when he said, "Everything nailed down is coming loose."

One expression of a search for stability and meaning in the late nineteen forties and nineteen fifties took the form of a semireligious revival. Church membership grew. Denominations commenced extensive building programs. Tens of thousands of young people flocked to summer religious camps and conferences. There was Billy Graham electrifying even New York City with sermons on the meaningful life while, in another sphere, Norman Vincent Peale advanced our "peace of mind." The meaning sought and the meaning offered in the religious upsurge of the nineteen fifties may have been sharply personal; obviously it demonstrates a grasping at something life needs: meaning and coherence.

At times we quest for meaning and coherence in individualistic ways; at others through social movements. We turn to religion, to sociology, to psychiatry, to materialism for answers. We put the world together with this theory today and that theory tomorrow. We long for the illusive, never quite located, "golden age" to restore. We project our utopias, then announce that no matter how bad it is only the present counts. The First Great Awakening of the eighteenth century and the Second Awakening of the nineteenth, the heady reform movements that punctuate our past, the drive for social unity in post–Civil War years, and the thirst for personal unity today are all, in some respect, expressions of the quest for meaning. And so it has been throughout American history and, I might venture to say, throughout human history.

What's it all about? What makes life worth the effort? What holds it together? How do we create, discover, or come by meaning—and hope? Old questions, still with us.

"In the beginning God created . . ." With those words from Genesis boldly before us on a movie screen, the North American Congress of the Laity began.

We used those words from the ancient Hebrew creation story for more than poetic reasons. They were an affirmation made by those of us who convened the congress. We had invited a diverse group of persons to come together for the purpose of exploring theology, culture, and their interaction under the theme "Divine Creation: Human Creativity," but we wanted to clearly state what we believed to be the overarching context.

It matters quite a lot in considering creativity, meaning, and hope whether one believes the whole of creation as we know it was made by the God of eternity-unto-eternity or by some thermonuclear accident. In an accidental universe, any meaning is most likely also accidental. If caprice made the world, caprice rules it.

"In the beginning God created . . ." We wanted to twist no arms theologically but to affirm with Christians of all ages that our faith tells us a divine power not containable by our philosophic systems or our religious categories made everything. How God created creation is not the issue. The issue is that in confessing all origin in God we also confess that everything that exists, and anything we do or make, say or toy with in our minds, can properly be interpreted only with reference to God *the* Creator. Gerald Ford, in his remarks on opening the congress, cited a Gallop Poll showing that while 94 percent of all Americans say they believe in God, three out of four make no connection between religion and their judgment on right and wrong. God created: not only are

God and ethics connected, despite what three-fourths of the Americans think, but human creativity, meaning, and being itself are inseparable from the Alpha of Alphas.

The congress theme passage from Scripture was Colossians 1:15–20, printed at the start of Part I of this book. This selection from the Pauline writings offers a specifically Christian understanding of the Creator. Christ, according to Paul, incarnates, gives form to the invisible God. No longer is the face of God hidden. No longer, Colossians says, does the Creator address humanity indirectly. God's Word, the divine revelation, has taken human form, has transformed humanity, and this power, this Christ, is the same that created and fulfills all things, so says Colossians. The key sentence is verse 17: "He [Christ] is before all things, and in him all things hold together." Transcendence becomes immanent. What does this mean for individual lives? For human societies? For hope and despair, and for meaning itself? What does it signify for the here and now, "the until . . ."?

The congress Bible study exploring the transcendence-immanence motifs in the first chapter of Colossians was unlike that of either a seminary course or a Sunday school class. We did not delve into the complications of Greek verbs or pass around the text, each person reading a verse. On three mornings, we listened to a different speaker interact with the passage in terms of some dimension of the creation-creativity theme. Then congress participants divided into numerous conversation groups to share reactions, objections, and personal insights. Form and content of the "theoquest" presentations were left to the speakers, although we intentionally invited individuals who would bring varying approaches. Martin Marty used a script and slides to examine "The Immanent Christ and Human Creativity." Bishop Festo Kivengere preached a sermon on "Creativity and Transcendence." And Eugene Kennedy gave a talk on the experience of "sacramental moments" in everyday life.

I have included the addresses of Kivengere and Kennedy in this first part of the book (Marty's is in Part III) and, in fact, they suggest the title "God, and the Ordinary."

Kivengere issued a stirring call to Christians to acknowledge that the transcendent God of Scripture is not a distant potentate but the very cement of the created order. He struck cords of response in the audience with his description of how we human beings reach . . . reach . . . reach out for something to give us "authentic existence," to fill the gaps of despair and take away the dread of death—reach for but never find except in God. He brought fresh language to Christian doctrine. Instead of lapsing into a phrase such as, "God became incarnate," he declared: "So in Jesus Christ, you see transcendence taking on legs, taking on a heart, taking on humanity." How marvelous to imagine God taking on legs. What a refutation of any theology that sees Christ as only a heavenly being fluttering through our world, as though nails did not hurt his hands or stones bruise his feet. And the bishop offered pointed reminder that in this world human rights are intrinsic because they flow from the nature of the transcending God who took on legs.

The Ugandan Anglican prelate, an evangelist and ecumenist, has only recently become widely known in America.. His freedom to visit with us, however, results from tragic circumstances that exemplify human bondage. After the assassination of Archbishop Janani Luwum in 1977, Bishop Kivengere was forced to flee the henchmen of Idi Amin in order to serve his Lord. While grieved by what has befallen Uganda and by his inability to serve his diocese directly, he steadfastly refuses to hate Idi Amin, who reportedly is responsible for the deaths of countless thousands of Ugandans. "I love Idi Amin," he says in conversation and in a book of that title. The bishop speaks these words, which surprise our sense of revenge, as a Christian convinced that God's love extends to every person, even a tyrant with bloody hands. If there were ever an example of despair being redeemed by hope, it is Festo Kivengere's attitude toward Idi Amin.

Kennedy's presentation, here entitled "Taking on the Human Condition," touches squarely on the issue of life's meaning and how it is experienced. Pyschologist and influential figure in modern pastoral counseling, Kennedy illu-

[31]

mined for the congress, as he has done for readers of his popular books, those ordinary moments in which we encounter the meaning of hope and love—those occasions when we learn to yield ourselves, to face separation and rejection, to wait. His blistering indictment of a culture that thinks the mysteries of life can be packaged for quick sale brought chuckles, cheers, and tears.

The possibility of encountering the divine creativity, the divine patience, the divine hope in the ordinary ins and outs of life surfaced repeatedly in the dialogues following the keynote addresses. At one point, Peter Berger called attention to the Christian's amazing, and paradoxical, ability to face everyday frustrations and agonies knowing they cannot be magically transformed yet seeing them as hopeful and redemptive. Thomas Howard, another of the "theoprobe" panelists, has written a moving book called *Splendor in the Ordinary,* a lyric venture through the home where love is taught and practiced. Despite the secularization of life, Howard maintains it is possible in the home to still "walk daily among the hallows." The commonplace, he says, both cloaks and reveals the holy: "We live in a dark age, and somewhere in this murk there has got to be lights burning in shrines and on altars, bearing witness to the presence of the holy." [1]

Kivengere's sermon, in chapter 1, rejects any claim that changes in human structures can produce authentic, meaningful life. It offers transcendence as the light in which all human problems can be sorted out and set right. At the same time, the bishop points to certain inalienable rights based not on ability, status, or constitution but on humanness itself. He urges Christians, because they know the cross, to heal wounds, overcome injustices, and build bridges of understanding.

The address by Kennedy, in chapter 2, ends with a challenge to have the vision to "care for the future of humanity."

Recognizing and working for human rights and otherwise

---

[1] Thomas Howard, *Splendor in the Ordinary* (Wheaton, Illinois: Tyndale House, 1976), p. 13.

caring for humanity automatically introduces the issues of human organization—politics, economics, cultural expressions. Few people, Christian or not, can conceive of beatitude arising from anarchy. How do Christians relate to and conceive of God relating to "the kingdoms of this world"? How do Christians relate to and conceive of God relating to Western civilization? To the nations of North America?

Several speeches and a lot of discussions at the Congress of the Laity focused on Western civilization (especially America) vis-à-vis the dominant role Christianity has had in our religious past. Is our society hopelessly secularized? What, if any, contribution can individual Christians or the church make to social-political improvement? Are there correlations between the will of God and national policies?

Three out of four Americans may draw no connections between religion and their decisions on right and wrong, but Christian images and language are woven into the very fabric of our political structures and cultural heritage. Do "freedom," "goodness," "justice," and "righteousness" have any meaning in public life and popular culture? Does America have a calling to high purpose in the world?

Former president Gerald Ford, honorary chairman of the congress, made brief opening comments that sum up one typical American point of view on how Christians should relate to society and nation. Ford's speech, in chapter 3, appeals to the laity to integrate personal commitment to Christ with "faithful thought and action—not just in our homes but in our national life." Faith and "positive Christian social action," he says, "go hand in hand." He goes on to affirm America's ability to solve many of humanity's afflictions: "It is God's work, as well as ours. We must be instruments in his hands."

Many, perhaps most, Americans are optimistic about the nation and the capacity of good intentions and hard work to overcome anything. This optimism cuts across party, religious, and racial lines. We may complain about virtually everything but, deep down, most of us care a great deal about America. Some of the harshest, and most prophetic, criticism of national shortcomings comes from persons, such as

Martin Luther King, Jr., who want not to destroy but to improve "the land of the free." We even like to say ". . . one nation under God."

Malcolm Muggeridge offers an entirely different message about the prospects of Western civilization in the address, in chapter 4, that closed the congress. He dismisses America as a model of the good, meaning-filled and, possibly, righteous society. No hope, no Christian hope here, he says. He finds no real freedom in America. Freedom for what? ". . . so that they could sleep with whomever they wanted to sleep with, male or female, break a marriage and enter into another just as the fancy took them, choose any one of an ever-increasing variety of television programs, abort an inconvenient birth, stupefy themselves with drugs, immerse themselves in porn . . ."

Muggeridge sees consumerism as America's religion and thinks repentance and conversion quite unlikely. He generally despairs of human institutions, systems, and political ideologies. His answer to the meaning question, his source of hope, is put in terms of participation in the divine purpose expressed in spiritual terms.

Chapter One

CREATIVITY AND TRANSCENDENCE

Festo Kivengere

"Creativity and Transcendence," what a phrase! The Christian faith suffers from long words; beautiful words, but they are worked to death, and usually so neutralized that when we hear them we are aware of a great distance between us and them. And particularly now, *transcendence,* which has to do with human beings and our relatedness to the One who is higher, greater, more perfect, timeless, limitless. What I have to say about transcendence is based on verses from Colossians 1. Paul wrote to the Christian people of Colossae, speaking of Christ:

> He is the image of the invisible God, the first born of all creation; for in him all things were created, in heaven and on earth, visible and invisible, whether thrones or dominions or principalities or authorities—all things were created through him and for him. He is before all things, and in him all things hold together. —COL. 1:15–17

The Colossians were invaded by all kinds of philosophies, not bad in themselves. The philosophies actually represented the search for reality, the search for fullness, the search for completeness. That search was the human game then, as it is our game today. To search for reality and meaning is part and parcel of us—human beings. We reach out and pull back and reach again. Often in reaching, we grab a person or a thing, then let go. We dance or jump with joy, then fall down. The psychiatrists in this country know better than the preachers about the incompleteness and dis-

[35]

cord that makes people reach out to reality. Their offices are packed with people confessing, "I am split in two." Psychiatrists try to bring the split together. Bless them! Pray for your psychiatrists! They have a tremendous ministry to bring these split personalities together.

The search for reality, for the Colossians and for us, is a reaching out to the transcendent. Psychiatry can really only analyze the problem. When it comes to recreating the fragmented life, it takes that unique One, Jesus Christ. Paul knew that as he wrote to the Colossians. First, the apostle says, in verse 17, Christ is the transcendent foundation, there all along as the basis of human creativity and existence. That is, Christ was *before all things*—before not in time but in superiority and preeminence. Transcendence is not some meaningless abstraction. No, in Christ is the basis of all things in nature, all things social, all things political, all things economic, all things religious. Second, *all things hold together*—cohere—in Christ the foundation. All human activities keep falling apart until they are brought together by the dynamic power of the love of Christ—the love stronger than death, the love that heals brokenness and brings creativity out of chaos.

My basic message, the message of Colossians, chapter 1, is that transcendence is the foundation of all things and the cohesive power holding together all creation and the human experience. Unfortunately, it is a message often pushed aside.

THE TRANSCENDENT DIMENSION: HISTORICALLY

A constant battle has raged in human thought over the authenticity of the human person apart from anything external. The quest for "identity" has exercised keen minds throughout the centuries. Religion, with its stress on the transcendent dimension of man, dominated the anthropological understanding for a long time. "Anthropos," the Greek word for man, means the "upward-looking one," since the human physical frame seems to point beyond itself. There is a kind of upward outreach even in man's posture.

But man's creative gifts posed many unanswered questions. He has always been his own greatest puzzle: What is man's authentic, his true nature?

In Christianity and Judaism, and in other related religions, man is the one to whom God speaks in an absolute and personal way. He is created in the image of God and commissioned to act creatively and authentically—that is, in freedom—as a being-in-relation-to the transcendent Lord of creation.

Conflict in man as a person and in his creativity began, according to the biblical revelation, when he reversed the order of creation, rejecting his relationship with the transcendent God in favor of an egocentric, material-centered existence. This is what the Bible calls "the lost sheep" experience or what theology calls "the fall of man."

Christianity brought the message of restoration. When God became a human person in Jesus Christ, that was transcendence coming lower and lower—cautiously, compassionately, understandingly into the creatures made in the image of the loving God. God never folded his arms and let the world go its way in fragmentation. The discord pained God, who acted in love at the creation. He acted in love in coming to restore the fragments of broken lives in a broken world. So in Jesus Christ, we see transcendence taking on legs, taking on a heart, taking on humanity. Isn't that "good news"? God was not afraid to come into the fragments! God in Christ came to restore harmony. The early Christians proclaimed to the world: "The lost transcendent dimension has been restored!"

DENIAL OF THE TRANSCENDENT DIMENSION

In the Middle Ages, between the ninth and the seventeenth centuries, scholasticism established a systematic perspective on the harmonious universe. All the sciences operated in a coordinated relationship, and man was securely at the helm of things. That system was cracked, beginning with Descartes (1596–1650), who introduced "doubt philosophy," which says that the only direct evidence man has is the certainty of the "I." Descartes' dictum was, "I think, therefore I am." Thus, for philosophy, the transcendent relationship between God and man was lost. Only the ego in isolation was left at the center of human life, and man was allegedly set free from domination by the world.

Immanuel Kant, in the eighteenth century, added to the emphasis on the "I" in Western philosophy. "I," said Kant, represents man's ability to know and "I" must be left alone by all things external in order to find happiness in the self. "I" is the true reality. God is no longer needed to bring man into being; rather, man thinks God into being! God is not encountered in the shock of an experience but is put into the background to be used in soothing the conflicting experiences of life.

One modern school of thought after another continues the search for authentic existence, most of them denying the transcendent dimension, many of them extremely individualistic.

Extreme individualism prepared the way for the Marxist philosophy and revolution, which make much noise about authentic, unalienated man. Marxism wants an economic, collective man whose identity is provided by a relationship to the history of economic forces and who is, therefore, a phantom—an ideal! Man becomes the effect, not the cause, of social and economic structures. Thus, man's troubles are not found in himself but in the structures that must be set right to set man right. In its attack on capitalism, Marxism says, "Change the structures, and man will change!"

TRANSCENDENCE AND HUMAN IDENTITY

The tragedy of the "I" philosophies and of Marxism is that they neither find nor restore man. Man, in fact, is always being lost when transcendence is rejected. Without the transcendent dimension, man is no longer personal. True human identity is lost or found depending on the relationship to something below or above. Is man related to things material? Then his worth goes down to material things. Is he related to the One above him, the God of his creation? Then man's worth is high and his authentic identity is protected by the divine presence. He is no longer devalued—a thing of utility to be discarded. He is and remains a dignified person before the transcendent God who gives him unchanging value. Here the transcendent brings out the intrinsic value of the human person created in the image of God. The authentic identity of the human person is to be in the image of God. Discard the transcendent and the human person is discarded, for it is in transcendence that the divine clue to human value is found.

There is no authentic humanity in the autonomous self. In the autonomous self there is a dwarfed, devalued, self-centered man, whose world has shrunk, who sees men and women like trees walking and fellow human beings as means to an end. In Marxism, for instance, man is useful for the state and is thrown away when no longer useful. In capitalism, persons are useful as they bring profit to the company or to the society and are put on the shelf when they are no longer profitable.

Who are we? It depends on what we are related to.

TRANSCENDENCE AND HUMAN RELATIONSHIPS

Only as each of us sees fellow human beings standing before God do we recognize the inalienable rights of others: the right of another to life, to live where he chooses, to speak and move freely. In the presence of God, every man, woman, and child is a VIP. The presence of God humbles us but never debases or devalues us. The clue to the discovering of human brotherhood lies in the restoration of our transcendent relationship. Coming back to the presence of God in Christ means coming back to our alienated brother and sister.

In Christ, all men and women are equal—not equal in gifts or statures, but in their intrinsic humanness. Racial differences, cultural differences, language and status no longer form the criteria for assessing the value of the human person; nor do they form barriers for isolating men from men. They form bridges across which we meet each other. The transcendent glory of the Lord lifts us above distractions to a place where all is light and love.

The Cross of Christ stands in the center of the human arena with all its conflicting scenes. It stands as the divine demonstration of the love that bridges the gulfs between men. The cross demonstrates two dimensions of God's love, namely: the transcendent dimension—God's loving breaking through to man in self-sacrifice; and the all-embracing dimension—God's love bringing man into friendship not only with God but also with his fellowman.

Both dimensions of God's love were experienced by Paul on the road to Damascus, and from then on he proclaimed the Christ of the Cross with great enthusiasm. Some of Paul's glowing expressions make our own Christian faith seem colorless in comparison:

> For all of you who were baptized into Christ, have clothed yourselves with Christ. As a result there is neither Jew nor Greek [race]; there is neither slave nor free man [class]; there is neither male nor female [sex]. You are all one in Christ Jesus!   —GAL. 3:27–28

Paul in Galatians is not talking about the classless society where all tensions have been eliminated through social services, or of ideal standards of living achieved through capitalism. He is speaking of harmony in diversity, where tensions and differences are redeemed from self-destruction and made creative.

TRANSCENDENCE AND PROGRESS

"Progress," what a charming word; it carries a fascinating attraction—a hope for the better! It is a beckoning ideal motivating action for improvement and forward movement. But progress to what? To where? If progress loses its goal, it becomes its own goal and loses its control and balance, consuming itself by boring repetition.

It is the transcendent dimension—"in Christ"—that gives progress a human face and a meaningful direction. Progress is saved from dehumanization only as it is directed toward him from whom comes the light shining in the darkness of our history. Progress must be kept under the control of God's love.

Our times are gripped by a "progressaholic" fever. The smogs of our technological advance have so blurred life's horizon and disfigured man's face that we have lost our fellowmen and are left with threatening shadows. Do we see the human beings in the office, the clinic, the political campaign, in the club and in church? Only as the dehumanizing smog of selfishness is lifted can we find each other and the true direction of human progress.

TRANSCENDENCE AND DEMOCRACY

As far-fetched as it may sound to political theorists, transcendence is the only common denominator for democracy. "A government of the people, by the people, and for the people," the dictum used by the founders of this great nation, has become the password of all who seek a fair way of keeping power under authority for creativity. But in the name of so-called "democracy," thousands have died and tens of thousands are rotting in the dungeons of this world.

Problems arise when we try to make a democratic society work without a relationship to the transcendent God. Apart from the Source from which it derives its dynamics, even democracy is bound to let us down, to leave us frustrated and groping for props. Paul, in Colossians, says "all things hold together in Christ" and that includes all things social, political, and economic.

The divine source of government is stated in Genesis. God created male and female in his own image. Why? Simply out of his uncalled-for love. Thus, humanity was created of love, by love, and for love, and this covers past, present, and future, and it covers the structures of society. It is only when democracy is set in the orbit of God's love that it is able to survive. Otherwise, hunger for power will corrode its essence and fill it with fear of the unpredictable, and fear unleashes destructive forces upon the world. The transcendent dimension can hold a democracy together and make it a service to mankind. Christ is crucial for democracy.

TRANSCENDENCE AND NATURAL RESOURCES

It must be obvious that misuse or overuse of our God-given natural resources has inevitable negative consequences. Predictable results follow certain actions just as night follows day. Scarcity follows waste. Hunger for wealth has led to the destruction of the elephant population in parts of Uganda. More ivory, fewer elephants. And so in other areas: more pollution, less fresh air.

Only as we discover the divine, gracious provision for us in the resources around us can we recover a balanced style of living and also discover that life is more than goods. The essence of real life is not in things. Paul in his letter to the Philippians (4:11–13) says, in effect, that he has learned the secret of living: I am no longer dominated by the fluctuating trends of things. I can live under all circumstances without succumbing because of the ability Christ gives me.

While things are not the essence of life, we need to make wise use of the resources God has made available. The hungry, the unclothed, the suffering, and the lonely refugees in an alien world need to feel the heartbeat of their fellowmen in practical outreach. But prosperity can make us drunk, and insensitive. Christ is trekking through the lonely and dangerous places of this world alongside his displaced brothers and sisters. And we should join in his great "operation rescue."

TRANSCENDENCE AND EACH OF US

The Cross of Jesus Christ is where you and I come and stand in front of that remarkable, incredible love and discover—you and I—that we are each unique because each is uniquely loved. The love of God singles me out—singles you out—bringing deliverance from confusion, from racial tensions, from destructive ideas, from selfishness, and loves each person. And in Jesus Christ, all of us, all humanity, hold together. Human problems can be sorted out if we stand in front of that almighty Cross.

Chapter Two

TAKING ON THE HUMAN CONDITION

Eugene C. Kennedy

"Creativity" is a word in our age that has come to be abused so that its original strength, the fire of the concept, has been banked and, like so many other profound words, it has been homogenized, made shallow, and trivialized to some extent by being overused. It is to return to a sense of the word's vibrance, to acknowledge personal commitment to its values in the Gospels, and to understand the meaning of recreating the face of the earth that we think together here.

It is unfortunately true, however, as we look around our culture we may feel that the majestic phrase from Scripture, "Behold, I make all things new" (Rev. 21:5), has to be read with a slight alteration. With the trivialization of creativity, it seems better to say, "Behold, I have made all things the same."

The invention of plastic may have been a sin against the Holy Spirit. We live in a world of reproductions, every one exactly the same; a world of echoes, reruns, and the threat of being able to preserve forever our favorite television show on a cassette, to be played at a later date. It is not just in entertainment that this is true. There have been predictable responses fashioned even in areas full of mystery. Americans, as we take up other challenges, also take up the challenge to tame mystery. And so mysteries such as love, intimacy, and trust are sometimes packaged into a weekend. We can see that the longing to understand these things is ill served by trying to mass-produce them. They will not yield their secrets so easily.

Death is one example of a central mystery that we have recently tried to organize, as we like to organize things in this country. We have instituted high school courses in which students design their own funerals, visit mortuaries and graveyards so that death becomes a friend instead of what it will always be—a half-understood and mysterious visitor. Death is far stronger than the ways we have tried to homogenize it, but still we try to order the mystery. Even in pastoral counseling we find precast phrases and a determination that people die in an orderly fashion, that they go through the various phases according to the counseling book.

Life and death are too strong for such treatment, and this kind of attitude toward creativity is the very death of it. We look at life, or we look at the Bible, and our understanding of it, in a more vital way when we open ourselves to mystery and give up our efforts to master every situation. We cannot get life down perfectly. Life is not an illness. Although many seek a cure, or turn to the latest book or prophet for treatment, life is something far richer. It is with life in this mysterious sense that we are concerned—with the creative powers that reflect the very essence of God.

TWO IMPULSES

Every institution, churches included, is caught between two impulses. In the church, one impulse is to organize, to put order into human experience, to make moral judgments and rules. The other impulse, partaking far more of the creative-mysterious strain, is to be a source of sacramental understanding, to illumine human experience. Two impulses: On the one hand to master experience and on the other hand to push away the darkness; on the one hand to control; on the other to free. Freeing is difficult and risky, so there is always tension between the impulses. Our interest is in a rediscovery and a reassertion of the creative impulse of the church. It is through the church's sense of tradition that creativity must be traced back to human relationships in our sacramental heritage.

[45]

What goes on in life? What takes place and where? Dr. Elisabeth Kubler-Ross, a marvelous student whose insights into death have suffered from the homogenization process mentioned earlier, gave an illuminating interview on what people talk about as they stand in the shadows of their own deaths. What do they remember about life? What is it they want to tell somebody else about life? The answer isn't how much money they had or how far they went on it, or how many coats they had or the size of their house. Rather, people want, as they reach the plane before death, to speak about simple things—things that might otherwise be forgotten: a beautiful day with their children, a trip they planned and finally made, a hike in the woods, some moment when they felt present in life with another. These are the sacramental moments out of which we create life. These are the moments that the churches are called to underscore so that people can look in the right directions for the sources of meaning in existence. Such moments, seemingly too simple, too ordinary to remember, offer us the key to the mystery of living, the key to the sources of creativity and sacramental understanding.

LIFE IN THE GAPS

The human potential psychology that, laudably enough, wants people to grow, has a kind of overeager enthusiasm that lacks the tragic sense that emphasizes simple moments. It emphasizes peak experiences, and most people have very few peak experiences in a lifetime. Most of us live in the valleys or are climbing the heights. We live, as the prophet Ezekiel said, in the gaps between then and now, trying constantly to bridge the imperfections of human existence. That, of course, is why the primary Christian virtues take on profound meaning—why we can understand something of the similarity between the simple gospel rhythms and the essence of creativity itself. The same dynamics are engaged in life and in the creative process, which is why the simplest of moments can be so majestic when seen in proper perspective.

In life and in the creative process, we must first take on the human condition with its limitations, have some sense that peak moments are rare and cannot be grabbed, know that life is not an illness waiting for a successful treatment. But the human condition can only be taken on if we enter into life. That means committing ourselves to this imperfect pilgrimage that we make together, if we are going to make it at all, and accepting this incarnation just as the poet or artist accepts the task of making flesh of some creative vision.

YIELDING OURSELVES

We are all challenged to die. We will be crucified. We will face death in a thousand small ways, even in these ordinary moments of trying to believe in hope and to love one another. We have to learn to yield ourselves up, even as artists yield themselves up to their visions of suffered diffusion. As one poet put it, he had to learn to give himself away so that the power in his process could become very exact. Through faith we know that death is not the end. The energies, the dynamics of the creative process are the same because we reach, through death, this giving away of the self, to resurrection, to a larger life for others and a larger life for ourselves.

We make purchase of meaning through this process repeated a hundred times in an ordinary day, repeated when we have to believe in each other after we have disappointed each other. Belief is not something impossible; it is far more challenging. Belief asks us to commit ourselves to what is possible about each other. That is what a husband and wife must do even after they have learned that neither is quite the person the other had expected and that, perhaps, they will not reach that peak moment they had envisioned.

Hope requires the same kind of readiness to die as we reach out to others, as we reach out to children as parents or to our pupils and give up something of ourselves rather than take from them. If resurrection is to be the term of it, love requires a readiness to yield up ourselves in a reciprocal fashion. Death must be undergone in order for the life to be full. A culture that tells us that these things can be bought or studied or mastered easily betrays God's creation and the very rhythms that finally deliver to people a sense of meaning. Some people have learned to take on the human condition, to die and then to rise again feeling they have lived. They may bear scars, but they never doubt that they have touched the deep and most mysterious and meaningful parts of their existences.

THEOLOGY IN THE EVERYDAY

The things we talk about in theology are not rare occurences but are of the very creative warp and woof of everyday for people who are trying to respond to one another in this imperfect world. What need would there be for love in a perfect world, where one would never fail in trust, never disappoint? Love is the response to the ragged edge of the human situation, the breach we must cross when we die the death. It is in revealing this kind of love to the world that we are most fully engaged when we commit ourselves to the sacramental realities of the Christian vision. Then some of the mysteries that seem so distant or seem merely to be theological categories become clear to us.

When we say "revelation," we remember God speaking to the prophets and to the early church and its leaders, but the Spirit speaks also to us, and we have all been in the midst of this very process. This is the religious experience of our lives. When someone loves us, when they reveal something of themselves to us, we see more of them, but something else happens. By the light of their revelation of themselves we not only see more of them, but we can see more of ourselves as well. And in this reciprocal process of enlarging each other's lives, there is a very real experience of resurrection: sometimes in very simple undramatic ways, in kissing and embracing after a misunderstanding, being able to understand a friend whose problems seem so complicated and twisted, in realizing that healing is far more significant, sacramentally, than standing in judgment against the world.

The gaps, as Ezekiel said, are the places where we discover what the mystery of our existence is all about.

SEPARATION

What are these sacramental moments that reflect so keenly the essence of the gospel dynamic and are the sources for our creating and recreating our lives? John Cheever has a touching story about a man who finds himself in the Indianapolis railroad station. His train is late, so he sits waiting in this old station and as he looks around he realizes that the railroad station was built, by design or by accident, much like a cathedral—vast distances and stained-glass windows and waiting-room benches shaped like pews. It puzzles him for a moment, but then he says, "Ah, yes, but how else could it be, for here is where we celebrate the mystery of travel and separation." It was no accident, of course, that railroad stations were built like cathedrals. So much of what was sacramentally significant in life took place in them; no accident either that our nostalgia for the age of railroad travel is not merely fascination with machines.

The railroad age recalls to us, perhaps only as a faint signal like a telegraph receiver late at night from far away, something that delivers meaning. Railroad stations, of course, are where people leave home for the first time in one of those first instances of the brief bittersweet taste of the mystery of separation that fills all our days; the railroad stations are where people come home after being away at college and come home changed, or come home after being at war and come home changed. The station is a place of comings and goings, of moments underscored because of those times we feel intensely everything that we mean to each other. If we cannot put it into words, we can feel it thoroughly throughout ourselves. This is an aspect of a mystery larger than railroad stations, but how difficult it is to feel the angularities of an airport where the mystery of travel is all but at a bitter end.

The mystery of separation is deep in our lives, even with

[49]

people who love each other very much. They cannot overcome separation. They must be apart, and the condition for
the freshness of their love is that they give each other
enough space to be separate. But how much dying goes into
that. It is a reflection of the separation of the body and
blood of Jesus in the Eucharist. We experience the Eucharist
ourselves in wanting people to be separate from us instead
of possessing them, in giving them their lives instead of trying to make them over as we would have them.

We learn to give ourselves away, and it happens in great
moments and in small moments. It happens when a husband
or wife leaves for work in the morning. We find it when husband and wife give a party. They share their love with their
friends and discover, at the end of an evening, they have
talked with everybody but each other. There is a strange
separation even in child rearing that makes parents reach
deeper into themselves to reach across it: a sacramental moment, the liturgy of life itself; and it is in such moments that
we redeem and are redeemed.

Take any other common experience: take beginnings and
endings. How full of the charged qualities of life they are,
because we are always beginning again and and we are
always coming to the ending of something. The year ends,
and we look backward to take some measure of it as another
one begins. We think we have proved ourselves for the last
time and then we must prove ourselves all over again. I am
the Alpha and Omega, the beginning and the end. Experiences that take place in initiative and experiences that take
place in termination deliver a perspective of life to us. We
speak of the beginning of a new phase in our life or the ending of a happy period in our life. We speak of the end of innocence, first words, last words, death itself—challenging us
not to manage but to face it with a creative force, love
stronger than death, that alone challenges it. We cannot look
away from death. These experiences fill all of our days.

Think of other moments that are familiar to all of us and
do not miss their profound religious significance. Familiar
moments are where we experience the mystery of living in
Jesus. What is more characteristic of human beings than

longing—longing for what, we cannot quite say but we feel a sense of absence and incompleteness, an ache in our hearts. The ache is not mindless but a signal of something deep and abiding and eternal about us.

Which of us, man or woman, young or old, does not face the mystery of rejection, of being misunderstood at a crucial moment, sometimes even by someone who loves us very much? Is there a deeper pain? Are there words to capture what we undergo? The Lord himself underwent it as the kind of death we must endure if we speak the truth, the truth so powerful and so free.

WAITING

Think of one last mystery. Waiting must be an awfully good thing because God put a lot of it in life. Think of all the waiting: the X rays are not back from the laboratory; the suit isn't ready; the parking lot is crowded; the dentist's office is behind schedule. What a mystery because the world says we aren't supposed to wait. This culture, which may die, as Norman Mailer said, its last testament the faint scent of a Xerox copy: this culture says, "Take gratification now. Do not delay. There is no need to put off anything, whether sex before marriage or any other kind of gratification, that you can get for yourself. Grab that gusto." A period of delay, a period of dying to oneself, is thought to be a sin, foolishness. Indeed, foolishness to this world, but there is no great work of art, no great love that has not been filled with waiting, with dying to oneself. All great love stories are filled with lovers who have to wait for each other.

Waiting, waiting sometimes for ourselves, saying, "I know I'm not ready for this yet"; waiting for someone else, a spouse perhaps, to reach the same point one has reached. Waiting, how full of pain it is. Sometimes we have to wait when we have hurt somebody else and we want immediately to seek their forgiveness. But the wound is too fresh, it stings too much, and we must wait in a cruel interlude before we can even be forgiven. Waiting is a mystery that surrounds us, that marks all of our days because we cannot achieve the light unless we are willing to undergo the death. That is why the churches have seasons of expectation and waiting in Advent and Lent. Waiting is not some mindless or terrible accident of the human situation. Rather, it is the way we experience sacramentally the ordinary things of our lives, the mysteries that give meaning to us and the mysteries that can give meaning to others.

In the musical play, *1776,* there is a moment near the conclusion in which the discouraged John Adams comes early to the convention hall where this dream, this creative dream of bringing the colonies together, seems to be floundering. He stands and addresses himself into the darkness of the audience, asking, "Is anybody there? Does anybody care? Does anybody see what I see?" As we approach the next century, man himself, men and women everywhere are asking similar questions: Is anybody there? Does anybody care? . . . Is our answer, "We are here, we have the vision and we care for the future of humankind"?

Chapter Three

GOD'S WORK—OUR WORK

Gerald R. Ford

Back in Michigan, the story is sometimes told of a farmer who was entertaining a minister at his home. As they sat on the farmer's front porch, the minister looked out on the hillside where a forest fire not long before had destroyed all the foliage and the vegetation.

"Well, I see that you have new scrub brush growing up there on the hillside," said the minister. "I'm afraid it doesn't look very attractive."

"You're right," replied the farmer. "It's not as pretty as it could be, but let me tell you something: It holds the world together."

And so it is with the church. Sometimes, as we look out, we may see things about organized religion that are not wholly to our individual liking, but let us always remember: The church holds our world together.

For some time it has been whispered that the church is philosophically defensible but practically irrelevant. Even the Gallup Poll last spring (1977), which indicated that America "is the most religious country on earth," alluded to the problem:

——94 percent of the American people believe in God;
——Four out of ten attend church or synagogue weekly;
——Only 6 percent indicate no religious preference.

But it goes on to indicate, when read thoroughly, that "although the U.S. is 'impressively religious' on the surface, a large gap exists between belief and practice. Three out of four do not connect religion with their judgments of right and wrong. God in his ethical dimension is denied."

The consensus would seem to indicate that religion is receiving mixed reviews, with polarization within the ranks. All of this at a time when opportunities for renewing our culture may be running out.

If it is true that the church of Jesus Christ is defensible but irrelevant, then my prayer is that this could change by a massive infusion of the creative Spirit of God. If the judgment about the church's relevance is not true, may the fallacy be exposed by a genuine renewal encompassing Bible study, evangelism, social action.

But however we perceive the church, we must each respond to this challenge with Christian integrity. This Congress of the Laity will, I sincerely hope, remind us again how much our civilization owes to Christian faith and how vitally important it is that our discipleship in Christ become the foundation of all that we do in our secular lives.

You may recall how the Apostle Paul wrote to the church at Ephesus many years ago: "Since . . . I heard of this faith of yours in the Lord Jesus and the practical way in which you are expressing it toward fellow Christians, I thank God continually for you. . . . God has placed everything under the power of Christ and has set him up as head of everything for the Church. For the Church is his body, and in that body lives fully the one who fills the whole wide universe" (Ephesians 1:15, 23. Phillips). I have always understood the Apostle Paul to be saying that Christ wants to live through us!

It should be like what happened when a little blind boy selling fruit in a busy train station was knocked over by a hurrying commuter. People continued rushing by on either side, but finally another harried businessman stopped to help the boy retrieve his coins as well as his fruit. As they were working together, the tearful boy asked, "Mister, are you Jesus?"

How wonderful it would be if in our everyday lives, all of us could express our faith in that way to our families, our businesses, our schools and our friends. . . .

More than a century ago, Abraham Lincoln told the story of an Eastern monarch who instructed his wise men to write for him a compelling sentence that would be true and appropriate in all times and situations. They presented him with the words: "And this too shall pass away."

Lincoln marveled at that very simple wisdom: "How much it expresses! How chastening in the hour of pride! How consoling in the depths of affliction!"

But how much greater still is the teaching of Jesus that, "The things of this earth shall pass away, but my word shall not pass away." (Luke 21:33)

I believe that, as Christians seeking to be extensions of his word, we are called upon to integrate our personal commitment to him with faithful thought and action—not just in our homes but in our national life.

Obedience to the call of discipleship requires that we, to whom much, much is given, concern ourselves with justice and practical service. Individual Christian salvation must be affirmed and brought to maturity by a healing involvement in our personal and social institutions. Faith and positive Christian action go hand in hand.

On both the right and left of our political spectrum there is a growing sense that the major issues of our times— human freedom, peace, economic progress, and the opportunity for personal fulfillment—all involve personal morality.

A strictly pragmatic approach to politics that leaves out questions of meaning and purpose is no longer possible. We can no longer keep our personal convictions in one compartment and our social beliefs and actions in a separate compartment. Instead, we must build a vibrant marriage of our faith in Christ with our works here in our own land.

That marriage would not be new to America. The spirit of Christ and of evangelism on our shores has long aroused concern for others in need. Many of our earliest institutions—our colleges and universities, our hospitals, and our children's homes—were a direct outpouring of a gospel ministry, of a spiritual awakening. . . . We are talking about a tradition that goes back many years in time. But all of us know that this tradition—this joining together of faith and good works—must be greatly renewed and revitalized in our own day. . . .

Frankly, I have always been an optimist. Our nation's strength and power, I believe, afford us the opportunity, never before known in history, to solve many of humanity's afflictions. We have the means at our disposal; I, for one, believe that we also have the will.

But much remains to be done and we cannot do it all alone. It is God's work, as well as ours. We must be instruments in his hands.

Chapter Four

HUMAN AND DIVINE RIGHTS

Malcolm Muggeridge

Curiously enough, it was while walking about the streets of Moscow in the early thirties that I first began to ponder upon what freedom meant, and what rights, if any, were vested in us just by virtue of belonging to the human race— what is called, heaven knows why, *homo sapiens.* I was doing a stint there at the time as correspondent for the old *Manchester Guardian,* then in the heyday of its reputation as the mouthpiece of the liberal mind at its brightest and best. Already I had come to realize, I must say with some inward anguish, the fraudulence of all the hopes I had entertained of finding the USSR a free, brotherly, prosperous, and peaceable society in process of being set up under the auspices of a dictatorship of the proletariat. Instead, I was confronted with an authoritarian government carried to a pitch far exceeding, for instance, the British Raj in India, my only previous experience of anything of the kind.

I spent a lot of time perambulating the Moscow streets and rubbing shoulders with the Muscovites similarly bent, this being the only unsupervised, unprogrammed contact with them permissible to foreigners. These people, after all, were the beneficiaries under the Revolution. In principle, their freedom and human rights were specifically and everlastingly guaranteed; in practice, they had neither freedom nor rights other than to read and think and believe and do whatever those set in authority over them considered appropriate. I found their anonymous presence oddly fascinating, and even appealing, aloof and remote as they were; so wrapped up in themselves, and, at the same time, a collectivity rather than a collection of separate individuals as in other towns I had known, like London or Paris. Mingling with them, I had a queer sort of almost mystical certainty, which remains with me to this day, that as they were, so we were all fated to be. In them, for those with eyes to see, might be discerned "the fearful symmetry of things to come." (William Blake)

THE BURDEN OF FREEDOM

It was not at all, let me hasten to add, that I envisaged the realization of the Marxist apocalypse of a triumphant proletariat taking over power and establishing themselves everywhere in authority; the final fulfillment of the promise in the Magnificat of the mighty being put down from their seats and the humble and meek exalted, of the hungry being filled with good things and the rich sent empty away. Only faculty members in the more distinguished history and philosophy departments, students with media aspirations and laicized Jesuits still entertain such expectations as that.

No, the feeling I had was something else; a sense that a phase of history was coming to an end, that Man, struggling to be free, with rights pertaining to his individual status, was going to give place to Man as part of a collectivity, a tiny digit in a huge total, and that in Moscow this new arrangement was being tried out and could be observed. There, as it seemed to me, a new serfdom was taking shape, which would set a pattern for the future. Thenceforth I have never doubted that a key to our present discontents is simply that the burden of being free has come to seem too heavy to be borne, and that, consciously or unconsciously, willfully or under duress, the prevailing disposition is to lay it down. In a famous scene in Dostoevski's novel, *The Brothers Karamazov*, the Chief Inquisitor turns away the returned Christ because he brings with him, as he had before, the dreaded gift of freedom. Governments, as it seems to me, whatever their ideology, are going to show themselves of a like mind with the Chief Inquisitor.

This view was reinforced by the truly extraordinary antics of visiting West European and American intellectuals for whom Moscow in the thirties was a place of pilgrimage, as Peking is today to their heirs and successors. They arrived there, an unending procession, ranging from famous figures like a Bernard Shaw, a Julian Huxley, an André Gide, a Lincoln Steffens, to crazed clergymen who could not keep away from the anti-God museum, driveling dons and Quakers, an occasional eccentric millionaire, miscellaneous actual or aspiring intelligentsia of every sort and condition, all concerned to do obeisance to a regime that, in its practice if not in its theory, represented everything they purported to abhor, but that nonetheless, they insisted, held out the prospect of enlarging human freedom and enhancing human rights for all mankind. The credulity with which they accepted at its face value whatever their guides handed out to them, provided a spectacle of rare comedy, and I cherish its memory as such. At the same time, it was a portent. If these, who at home were the ardent custodians of human rights and freedom, were so ready, even eager, when they were in the USSR, to throw them to the Kremlin wolves, what chance was there of defending them when, as they must, they came under attack as our turbulent twentieth century unfolded? Solzhenitsyn has immortalized this tragicomic scenario, this great betrayal by the Enlightenment's last legatees, in his hilarious account of an official visit by Mrs. Eleanor Roosevelt to a Soviet labor camp where he was incarcerated. At the time I could not, of course, envisage the final irony—that these very intellectuals would provide the style and manner of thinking of the pundits and gurus of the media, especially television, destined to hold the whole Western world in thrall—the Don Quixotes of the TV screen, who would charge so valiantly and vociforously against the windmills of Watergate.

AMERICA

Some fifteen years later I went to Washington, this time as correspondent for a Conservative newspaper, the London *Daily Telegraph*. In the intervening years there had been another devastating war, ostensibly fought for freedom and human rights, which involved accepting the Red Army as a liberating force and, at the Nuremberg war crimes tribunal, American and British judges sitting along Russian ones in condemning the defeated Germans for infringing human rights by partitioning Poland, which they had done in collaboration with the Soviet government under the terms of the Nazi-Soviet Pact, and for using forced labor, which continues to be a permament feature of life in the USSR—vide *The Gulag Archipelago*. The Germans were also convicted of infringing human rights by the practice of compulsory sterilization and euthanasia, whose legalization is now being recommended in Western countries on humanitarian and compassionate grounds. Thus it has taken just thirty years to translate a war crime into an exercise in humanity and reinforcement of human rights.

I came to Washington not at all in the ebullient mood of my arrival in Moscow, but even so there was a sense of excitement in venturing into what was still called the New World. Moreover, America at this time had a position of preeminence among other nations in terms of weaponry and wealth unparalleled in modern times. Phrases like "manifest destiny" were again being bandied about, and human rights were very much in, and on, the air, with the Freedom Bell tolling on all appropriate, and sometimes inappropriate, occasions. Roosevelt, for instance, had launched his Four Freedoms, one of which—Freedom from Want—appearing on the almost worthless currency notes circulating in Italy during the Allied occupation, caused considerable wry mirth among the local populace. Human rights, likewise, figured in numerous declarations, preambles, statements of intent, and solemn undertakings, as in the proceedings of the United Nations, which had risen, phoenix-style, out of the ashes of the old League of Nations, to be a more riddled Tower of Babel than its predecessor.

No people, it is safe to say, in all history have been so specifically and lavishly certified to be free and in the full enjoyment of all their human rights as the Americans. Yet, I asked myself, were their freedom and their human rights real or illusory? Certainly, as long as they had money, unlike the Muscovites, they could do as they pleased, read whatever they wanted to read, go wherever they had a mind to. Moreover, thanks to the Supreme Court and other judiciaries, their human rights were constantly being extended, so that they could sleep with whomever they wanted to sleep with, male or female, break a marriage and enter into another just as the fancy took them, choose any one of an ever-increasing variety of television programs, abort an inconvenient birth, stupefy themselves with drugs, immerse themselves in porn, and ultimately, if they so wished, just with the aid of a hypodermic syringe or some sleeping tablets, bring their days to an end. All this with the advertisers and the media making straight the way.

Was it freedom ever burgeoning or a servitude ever more exacting? Human rights or human fantasies? Seeking to answer, I turned to the American motorways as I had in the USSR to the crowded Moscow streets: six lanes to a side, and the endless stream of vehicles roaring along in both directions from nowhere to nowhere; the man at the wheel easefully surveying the ever-extending vista of tarmac, a cigarette drooping from his mouth, behind him a suit from the cleaners swinging gently to and fro on its hanger; the radio on, from Muzak to Newzak, and then back to Muzak, drooling tunes followed by drooling news, followed by more drooling tunes, and so on *ad infinitum,* the whole effect calculated to keep the driver's mind in a state of vacuity, and so receptive to the advertisements that regularly punctuated both Muzak and Newzak, urging him to eat this, wear this, anoint and perfume himself with this, tone up his bowels with this and tone down his body odor with this. Then, as the evening comes on and the tarmac darkens, the neon signs come out; each cluster of homes displaying the basic four—food, drugs, beauty, gas—the four pillars of the American way of life.

ANOTHER VIEW OF FREEDOM

Having now looked at two versions of freedom in contemporary terms, and the human rights that go therewith, the one a servitude to an all-powerful state and the other to an all-demanding ego, I turn to what the Apostle Paul called the glorious liberty of the children of God, the only true and lasting freedom there is, and the only basis on which human rights can exist at all and be valid. Words that, as St. Augustine woefully remarked, have a beginning and an end, are inadequate to describe this other freedom, deriving, as it does, from eternity and not from time, and carrying with it human rights as belonging to God's creation and so participating in his purposes, rather than with reference to any earthly laws or instruments. It was this freedom and these were the human rights that Solzhenitsyn discovered in what were in worldly circumstances the most abject imaginable—a Soviet prison camp. "It was only when I lay there on rotting prison straw," he writes, "that I sensed within myself the first stirrings of good. Gradually it was disclosed to me that the line separating Good and Evil passes, not through states, nor between classes, nor between political parties, but through every human heart and through all human hearts.[11] And he concludes: "So, bless you, prison, for having been in my life." Others, we may be sure, in the grisly Gulag Archipelago, will likewise have been discovering freedom and their human rights as being created by God in his image, while the representatives of governments were appending their signatures to the ludicrous Helsinki Agreement on Human Rights, and afterwards entering into interminable and meaningless discussions in Belgrade as to what the agreement's terms meant and whether they had been duly observed.

I love one other example of this discovery of freedom in the most adverse circumstances, which Solzhenitsyn also describes—the man in the bunk above his. This fellow somehow in that terrible place remained cheerful, remained brotherly, remained helpful to others. Solzhenitsyn observed that in the evenings, when this man crawled into his bunk, he pulled some pieces of paper out of his pocket and started reading them. They were sentences scribbled and, of course, came from the Gospels. I thought when I read this: Have any other sentences in all human history been written that could also have comforted and uplifted a man in that terrible place? Supposing they'd been sentences from the American Declaration of Independence or from the Fifteen Points of President Wilson or from the Charter of the United Nations. Do you imagine they would have given that man one minute's peace in the circumstances in which he was placed? That's what we have to remember—that we find freedom not in courts of law or in international declarations. We find freedom in our relations with our Creator and by the instrumentality of the Incarnation and the Gospels it recorded.

In the world of the motorways, too, the victims of that other servitude may discover their true freedom and human rights, rejecting all the different allurements of what the Pascal called "licking the earth," and hearing beneath the drooling Muzak and Newzak the clear sweet voice of human brotherhood and companionship with God. Suddenly caught up in the wonders of God's love flooding the universe, made aware of the stupendous creativity that animates all life, and of our own participation in it—every color brighter, every meaning clearer, every shape more shapely, every word written and spoken more coherent. Above all, every human face, all human companionship, all human encounters recognizably a family affair; the animals, too, flying, prowling, burrowing, all their diverse cries and grunts and bellowing, and the majestic hilltops, the gaunt rocks giving their blessed shade, and the rivers making their way to the sea—all irradiated with the same new glory. This is freedom—the sense of belonging to God's creation; these are our human rights—to participate in the realization of his purposes for it.

It is like coming to after an anaesthetic; reconnecting with reality after being enmeshed in fantasy, picking out familiar shapes and faces with delighted recognition. There is a kind of vision expressing this that has often come to me; an adaptation, I dare say, of Plato's famous image of the shadows in the cave. I find myself imprisoned in the tiny dungeon of my ego, fettered and bound hand and foot with the appetites of the flesh and the will, unable to move or to see. Then I notice that light is somehow filtering in, and I become aware that there is a window through which I can look out. Looking out, I see eternity bathed in the light of God's universal love. The window focuses this light as the Incarnation focuses God's love, thereby miraculously bringing it within the dimensions of time, and procuring my release. My bonds and fetters fall away, I break out of the tiny dungeon of my ego like a butterfly out of its chrysalis. I am free.

GOD'S MERCIES

One of the many pleasures of old age is to become ever more sharply aware of the many mercies and blessings God showers upon us. Almost every day I discover new ones. What joy, for instance, to be confronted with power and authority in disarray in all their guises everywhere! How reassuring and diverting to find all our egotistic pursuits being made to seem derisory! As the quest for money, by the presses that print more and more of it, and the Arab sheiks into whose artless hands more and more of it falls. As carnality, by erotomania and porn, the *reductio ad adsurdum* of sex, and accompanying sterility rites and inexorable drift into impotence. As celebrity, by the media that bestows it so lavishly on auto-cued newsreaders, cinematic beauty queens, miming pop stars and grunting prize fighters. As knowledge, by sociology and kindred studies, with their computers, public opinion polls, and other devices for making false deductions from incorrect data. I've always felt myself that the Romans were much more sensible people. When they came up against questions of the sort pollsters ask, they looked for solutions by dropping the entrails of a chicken on the ground and seeing how they fell. This seems to me a much more promising and scientific method. I could go on and on. If C. S. Lewis were alive today, he would, I feel sure, have Screwtape complaining to his lord and master, Old Nick himself, that there was scarcely one plausible vice left on the calendar.

Again, how thankful we should be that the two rival prospectuses for a man-made kingdom of heaven on earth, the Soviet model based on power and privation, and the American one based on affluence and self-indulgence, both come to look ever more unconvincing! Sixty years of what is called social engineering in the USSR and its satellite countries have only served to provide the most promising scope since the Dark Ages for proclaiming the good news of the Christian revelation. As for the pursuit of happiness—with the media to promote it and an ever-rising gross national product to finance it, still the psychiatric wards are overflowing and the roads to the East teeming with bearded and bra-less dropouts who resolutely refuse to join in. Just supposing, I have often reflected, God had handed over the gruesome task of exploding Marx's turgid dialectics by attempting to implement them, to the Germans and the Japanese instead of the Russians and the Chinese, how immeasurably worse our present plight would be! Likewise, if he had entrusted the British rather than the Americans with wealth and nuclear power abounding!

The other day the very charming and holy Archbishop of Los Angeles, Cardinal Manning, was kind enough to refer to me publicly as a prophet. I wanted to adapt the words of Amos when he was similarly categorized: "I am no prophet, nor am I a prophet's son; I am an herdsman, a gatherer of sycamore plants, and the Lord took me as I followed my flock," and say: "I am no prophet, I am a journalist, a collector of news stories, and the Lord took me as I sat at my typewriter." If, however, I were to venture upon an essay in prophesy, it would be this—whatever may happen to the nightmare utopias of the twentieth century, whether they mutually destroy one another or, metaphorically speaking, fall into one another's arms, however deep the darkness that may fall upon our world, of one thing we may be certain. In some forgotten jungle a naked savage will feel impelled to daub a stone with colored mud and prostrate himself before it, thereby opening yet another chapter in man's everlasting and indefatigable quest for God, making one more humble acknowledgement of the mystery of his existence and his destiny.

Keep in mind one single sentence from the Bible: "If God be with us, who can be against us?"

Chapter Five

WESTERN CIVILIZATION: HOPE OR NO HOPE?

The panel discussions (theoprobes) following the five keynote addresses were informal. The speaker, along with permanent panelists Peter Berger, Thomas Howard and Michael Novak, and Gary Demarest, the moderator, sat in swivel chairs on floor level, with the audience, in a tiered horseshoe looking out, or down, on them. Written questions were received from the audience for panel response during the third, fourth, and fifth sessions, an innovation suggested by several persons.

As I indicated in the Introduction, the forty-five minutes after Muggeridge's "If God be with us . . ." was filled with excitement. It pinpointed the paradox of heavenly-earthly hope struggling with despair and set forth some basic views on transcendence and immanence translated into the social-political sphere.

Peter Berger had the first question. The audience was animated from listening to the legendary Muggeridge. Berger toyed with his little cigar. "Well, Mr. Muggeridge, I admire you so much. . . . If you came out against shoes tomorrow I would start going barefoot. . . ." But Berger disagreed with much of Muggeridge's premise and application, and in an ever so gentlemanly way stated his problems:

"Yes, all societies and visions of societies are shabby compared to the freedom promised in the Christian Gospel. No, America is not perfect. Yes, some of the description of America is correct. No, totalitarianism in the Soviet Union or elsewhere is not attractive. But: ". . . the implication that

Americans are more materialistic than other people . . . is simply not true; . . . It is not helpful to suggest it really doesn't matter whether the two utopias (the US and the USSR) of our times fall into each other's arms or destroy each other or whatnot. I think there are enormous differences between the two. . . . I think that the freedoms, the decencies, that we have achieved, or are aspiring to achieve in our society, have a significance that is Christian."

Muggeridge agreed to the last point, with a stipulation. "Civilizations die," he said. "Our Lord cannot die and I have come to feel that the only things that I consider utterly and pledge myself to are the things that are eternal." He was not denigrating, he said, but simply pointing out the "buffoonery" of human efforts.

A question from a man in the audience, early in the conversation, asked, "I am urged by some to become involved in the political processes and, in the interest of society, to serve the present age and make this a better world, perchance to save it. But most voices tell me this would not matter, for the cause of Western society and culture is lost. I hear you, Mr. Muggeridge, to agree with those voices of cynicism of all man's efforts. . . . Am I correct?"

Muggeridge was bothered by the word "cynicism." "The word . . . is totally wrong. There are two points to this. Is Western civilization in its downward path? Has it reached a point of no return? That is a matter of assessment by an individual mind, based on the data that the world offers us. With regard to participation in the governing processes that citizens are part of it, it seems to be a matter of whether a person feels he could do some good there. . . . What would be fatal and break his heart would be if he went into politics thinking he could make the sort of kingdom of heaven on earth that politicians are always suggesting they can do."

Michael Novak wanted to know if Muggeridge was aware that his criticism of America played into the hands of Marxists and other radicals who say freedom in America is not real, only consumer freedom? Yes, Muggeridge was aware. Saying what one thinks, he said, often brings involvement with people one would not wish as associates. "Exactly the same thing has happened over my own poor efforts in England to stand against this dreadful pollution of pornography . . . , but I think that was true, for instance, of the Apostle Paul, as he went around denouncing the legalistic attitude to faith of Judaism. He would find himself in some very strange company, but it didn't mean he'd have to stop doing it. . . ."

The dialogue continued:

GARY DEMAREST: Someone [in the audience] is asking if you would comment, Mr. Muggeridge, on your feeling about the public image of Christianity in America in light of what is referred to here as "Sunday morning hucksterism," and I gather this refers to your graphic description of hucksters in every area of life. There is a certain amount of that in the field of Christian religion . . . in the media . . . What about the implications of selling Jesus as other products are sold?

MUGGERIDGE: . . . I am infatuated with the Christian faith and, therefore, I find, even at its most grotesque and debased presentation, it more palatable to me than the most highly cultivated presentation of . . . commodities. I can bear anything if behind it, however clumsily and inadequately and impurely marshaled, is the love of our Lord . . .

MICHAEL NOVAK: Isn't it possible to feel a kind of infatuation with, first, Western civilization and, second, the American experiment? . . . Is it possible for a civilization to be "born again"?

MUGGERIDGE: . . . I doubt it. . . . It seems to me that civilization is a worldly thing. . . . Our civilization came to pass with the Incarnation, but it has become a great structure of power. It's had two thousand years of history, it has produced fantastic achievements in the way of art and literature, glories that will never be lost, but then that is not to love it in the sense that one can love our Lord . . .

BERGER: . . . Of course, one cannot love Western civilization as we love our Lord. If we did, it would be an act of idolatry. How could one disagree with that? But yet we can love it and I think—I'll go one step further—I think there is a connection between the two loves in the sense that the things of this world are not only a mass of perdition. They also point us toward God. They are signals of something beyond themselves.

. . . .

NOVAK: . . . It seems to me there's an obligation upon a New World, a new land, a new people, as we call ourselves here [in America]. We're called the "last hope of humankind" and we [feel] bound to carry out the task of building a civilization as close to the Kingdom as we can, until we're released from the obligation. We can't give up in despair, because there is still so much hope for this country.

MUGGERIDGE: I don't want you to give up in despair, but . . . I just feel the venture is not a very promising one.

. . . .

BERGER: What does it mean for a Christian to be in the world?. That, it seems to me, is what this congress is basically all about—the laity in the world. People are not professionally concerned with religion but concerned with other things and, while we have been talking about civilization and politics and America, we could talk about worldly problems people have in their personal lives, whether it's with illness, or children, or frustrations at work. And I think there are always two things one can say as a Christian. One is what Mr. Muggeridge said very eloquently and very correctly, that in the end none of it matters but, on the other hand, until the end it matters a good deal.

. . . .

THOMAS HOWARD: . . . The definition of freedom which you [Muggeridge] set forth upon . . . seems to be at such a polar extreme from the notion of freedom at work in the enterprises we generally call "social justice" . . . There's almost a notion of the blessedness of poverty. . . . How radically do we understand the notion of the blessedness of poverty?. . . . If you lift everyone to a better level materially, are you leading them after a fox fire?

MUGGERIDGE: Well, I personally think you are. I speak as a man who has spent most of his life in a welfare state in which it is automatically assumed that improvements in the economic circumstances of men must make them better and, of course, the evidence is very much to the contrary. I will dare to say, and it does require considerable audacity to say it, there never was a truer word spoken than, "the poor are blessed." The poor are blessed because they are free by virtue of their poverty from the preoccupations which accompany great possessions, great power, great influence.

There was uneasy movement in the audience as Muggeridge spoke of the blessedness of poverty. Michael Novak told a joke, which helped to relieve the tension. Muggeridge responded with one. Berger pushed the point Tom Howard had raised:

We're still talking about what it means to be in this world, and I'd like to draw a connection between these political things . . . and personal and private things. Of course, any act to produce more justice is tainted. We know that. It often leads to consequences unforeseen and the opposite of what anyone hoped for. Nevertheless, I think there are moments in history when certain actions in the name of justice point to God's justice and, by that token, are lifted above the misery of this world. I think the moment in the sixties when this society was goaded by Martin Luther King, Jr., and others to redress the evils of racial discrimination and racial injustice was such a moment. Now, I think the same can be said of personal life: Tainted human acts can point to God's love. And I think what is distinctively Christian, as against most other religions, is this way of looking upon the ordinary world as at least potentially a sacrament.

MUGGERIDGE: I like that very much. I think I was wrong in being too dogmatic about poverty. . . . All I mean is the assumption that if you can make people comfortably off you will make them good, happy, and Christian is a gigantic fallacy.

Time ran out. The paradox of transcendent-immanent hope intersecting despair was as paradoxical as ever, but it had been illuminated. We can live with seeming contradictions we can see; it is the ones in the dark that drive us to the psychiatrist's office.

Part II

AT THE EDGES IN LIFE

But you are a chosen race, a royal priesthood, a holy nation, God's own people, that you may declare the wonderful deeds of him who called you out of darkness into his marvelous light. Once you were no people but now you are God's people; once you had not received mercy but now you have received mercy.

I PETER 2: 9–10 (RSV)

The ministry of reconciliation is accomplished by the whole Christian community as its members live and act in every walk of life in the world.

ARNOLD B. COME
Agents of Reconciliation

OVERVIEW

A few years back, a United Methodist group meeting at the Chicago Temple used "servants at the edges" as its theme in a service of thanksgiving for lives willingly dedicated to Christ in the world. "Servants at the edges" is a figure of speech especially fitting to lay witness and service. As a dramatic reading during the Chicago liturgy said, anything with edges has a center. For the man or woman of the Christian laity, faith in Christ, strengthened by the worship and fellowship of the church, is the center—the reference point and motivating thrust. But most of our time is spent and our energies expended outside the sanctuary. In the sanctuary, in our lay fellowship groups, it is easy to sing "How Great Thou Art" and "I Would Be True." Then, out there in the world of work, the world of school district disputes and high meat prices, we find ourselves humming, "O for a Faith that Will Not Shrink."

Faith is put into practice by the laity in the world—at the edges. Why make synonyms of "world" and "edges"? Should faith not be expressed and put to work in the middle of things? Of course, but the image of the "edge" is helpful in reminding us that our testimonies to Christ are never properly confined to the ecclesiastical intersanctums or to lay retreats. Our witness and service as laity is most urgently needed at the outermost limits where the Gospel is rejected or has never been heard. The well have no need of a physician, Jesus said. The calling of the laity is to the ministry of healing, reconciling love on all of those edges encountered in the work-a-day world, in the office, on the assembly line, at home, in political and economic affairs.

The "edge," furthermore, is a good metaphor for the world itself as we know it as Christians. This here and now is the edge between God's initiation of creation and redemption and God's fulfillment of love in the coming Kingdom. At the edge where faith and action come together we make a difference as Christian laity in the midst of the world.

Being in the world as lay Christians involves more than individual witness and personal acts of charity. To serve Christ who "holds all things together," we have a responsibility to come to grips with issues and systems and ideologies that challenge the creative resources of faith. W. H. Auden, in his poem "For the Time Being" speaks of the "kingdom of anxiety" through which we pass in pilgrimage to that great city awaiting us. So we do. And, to borrow another phrase from Auden, we encounter "rare beasts"—friendly and hostile—some of which bear such names as "politics," "poverty," "marriage," "justice and injustice," "racism," "medicine and health," "war and peace," and "parenthood." Making application of faith in Jesus Christ as we deal with such beasts is not only complicated; it is also testing. Easy answers there are not. The challenge calls for unity, for intellectual maturity, and for a willingness *as personal and social Christians* to engage big issues and the whole of the culture.

The Congress of the Laity set forth and explored some of the broad issues and cultural realities the laity encounters at the edges where the paradox of hope fights its battle with despair. We set forth more issues than we explored to any depth, and the following five chapters merely exemplify those considered in some manner. Four chapters contain and draw their themes from congress keynote addresses, with amplification and elucidation gleaned from workshops (theoventures). Here are Abigail McCarthy reflecting on both the "lay callings" and, as a writer herself, on the role of the arts in building human community; John P. Newport on the interrelationships of Christianity and artistic creativity, a topic that also highlights an intense congress interest in the use and misuse of communications media; James Reston on the connection between the individual and public morality, and Peter Drucker on the role of the organization in modern life.

The fifth chapter, on the family, is taken from a workshop presentation by Armand Nicholi, M.D., a psychiatrist and faculty member at Harvard Medical School.

No book of reasonable size could even summarize everything said in the twenty-four workshops or describe the creative emotions stimulated by the performing arts during the congress. The fact that we had workshops on poverty, ecology, evangelism, and politics, race relations, the women's movement, and humor but that no chapters on those topics appear here in no way reduces their importance. Physical arrangements prohibited the tape recording of some workshops and equipment fouled in at least one. Some formats did not lend themselves to a transfer of contents to paper.

My purpose in this section is to present a sampling of contemporary issues that call for the creative response of the Christian laity.

For life lived in God, the old Quakers had a beautiful word: to be "centered." John Milton, in the seventeenth century, said such a focus, in the midst of storms and darkness, enabled us "to sit 'in the center' and enjoy bright day." The modern laity in new ways is also learning the triune promise: Out at the edges we get drawn to the center again.

Chapter Six

LAY RESPONSIBILITY: CHURCH AND WORLD

A. RESURGENCE OF THE LAITY

Mark Gibbs, editor of the *Audenshaw Papers,* published by the Audenshaw Project in Laity Education, has wondered if 1978 might go down as "the year of the American laity." He cites the North American Congress of the Laity and *A Chicago Declaration of Christian Concerns* as evidence to support his speculation. Issued by a group of influential Roman Catholic lay leaders and clergy, the Chicago document charges the United States Catholic Church with failure to realize Second Vatican Council promises on lay mission in the secular world. It protests "obsessive preoccupation" with ecclesiastical structures and processes to the neglect of the unique ministry of the laity. "We are deeply concerned that so little energy is devoted to encouraging and arousing lay responsibility for the world," signers said.

My friend, Mark Gibbs, could, of course, have cited many other indications of a resurgence among the laity. Across the past few years, institutes and programs produced by or urging lay assertivism have flowered like violets in spring. Some are rejuvenated denominational, ecumenical, or evangelical agencies there all along. Others are organizationally new. Any person on religion-related mailing lists is sure to receive a couple of different flyers each month announcing a new training program for laity, a conference on lay theological education, or a new "here's how" manual for use in the congregation.

The laity is stirring, not yet fully awake to the meaning of Christian discipleship . . . and, of course, never asleep like some religiously corporate Rip Van Winkle. In fact, the language of sleeping and waking, or of stirring as contrasted with lying still, is actually inappropriate, too dramatic for what I see happening. What is happening, as I interpret it, is a widening and deepening of the laity's understanding of Christian responsibility. The traditional lay role in recent American decades has been limited both by what was expected and, more specifically, by what rank-and-file laity was willing to be and do, identified with Christ as the church out in the world.

Situations differ from denomination to denomination, but generally the major role of the American laity in this century has been to pay religion's bills. That is a hard saying but, unfortunately, true. We, the laity, get the bills for the pastors' salaries, for reroofing the Sunday school annex, for subsidizing the parochial school, for feeding the hungry in the name of Jesus, and for supporting the missionaries, evangelists, and church bureaucrats. And not only the church bills do we get. We also have put on our hearts those thousands of paraecclesiastical, religiously humanitarian, and soul-winning organizations, as numerous as the names in the Manhattan telephone book.

By and large, we of the laity are good and faithful footers of religion's bills. With self-sacrificial egg money and ego-boosting tax writeoffs, through pledges and out-of-pocket contributions, out of affluence and love of God, we keep the gigantic business of American religion working and I, for one, think we ought to go right on supporting it. But we ought to do more, much, much more than pay bills.

"Religion is too serious a business to be left to the clergy," James Reston said in a press conference at the Congress of the Laity, and he is right. Too often, decisions affecting Christian ministry, its definitions and styles, have been left to the clergy and to lay church professionals, the latter hardly distinguishable from the clergy in the minds of many everyday lay folks who do not "work for the church" in terms of receiving financial compensation. Again, polity differences matter. The Roman Catholic laity has not held and still does not hold as much leverage within church structures as is theoretically possible for the Protestant laity. But quite often within the Protestant denominations the "partnership" of clergy and laity is a myth, partly because on every level decisive influence is asserted by or afforded to the professionals. Furthermore, some of the democracy-minded denominations have a peculiar democratic practice: on regional and national levels one hundred thousand lay persons are represented by twenty-five lay delegates and four thousand clergy by twenty-five delegates.

I know, the free-church traditions are supposed to be exceptions, and I am aware that in certain times and places, such as colonial New England, the clergy has felt tyrannized by the laity. Still, even the congregational-polity churches have in recent years become clericalized, if by nothing more than efficient, personable ministers who keep the budget balanced and are not to be threatened lest St. Beulahland Baptist fall behind in its building fund.

Worse than any of the above is the degree to which church professionals have been allowed—or forced—to do most of the theological thinking and expected to do most of the "Christian" work. (Notable exceptions could be cited among churchwomen, especially in the missionary enterprise. Whether because they have had to fight so long and hard for recognition and were, until fairly recently, denied ordination in Protestantism, or because they have stronger inherent religious inclinations, women seem to have a keener awareness of lay responsibility than do men. Happily, groups of Christian women have for decades, and without so much as a "by your leave" to the bishops and presbyters, commissioned, distributed, and used study materials abounding in theological wisdom and highly sensitive to lay witness and service in the world.)

Expansion of the laity's understanding of Christian responsibility is bound to create tensions between lay people and the ministers. This, as I said in the Introduction, is one of the edges where reconciliation is needed. Let me stress and restress that the role of the laity can be broadened without a wave of anticlericism. The Congress of the Laity was at no time anticlerical. It is true that some local lay groups are today setting themselves up as congregations without benefit of clergy. More often, house-based worship and study augment and complement participation in a regular parish or congregation.

I personally detect little overtly anticlerical sentiment within the modern lay awakening. Of course there are anti-leadership dynamics in any organizational experience, secular or religious. But informed lay Christians know there are historical, theological, sacramental, and practical reasons for the ordained ministry. We want ministers to attend to their sacramental and pastoral obligations, to preach prophetic and nurturant sermons, and to fulfill whatever administrative duties are given them within the various denominational systems.

While it is, perhaps, inevitable, the tension between clergy and laity is painful to me because, since neither are second-class Christians, it pits "lay rights" against "clergy rights," a kind of thinking more kin to tyranny and resistance than to the church and its love. The issue is the strengthening of the whole Christian community and better preparation of the *laos*—the people of God—for Christian vocation in the world. If a better educated, more aggressive, and increasingly creative laity threatens the clergy, so be it, and let us work together in overcoming the problems. In the meantime, the laity has need to consolidate its energies and exercise its unfolding responsibilities, and that includes coming to the aid of overworked, underpaid, misunderstood pastors, searching with them for new levels of awareness, care, and unity, all together.

The Congress of the Laity was posited on a belief in the essential equality of clergy and laity, a point well made by Abigail McCarthy in the opening keynote address. The agenda was not geared to strategies for asserting lay power within ecclesiastical structures, although as Mrs. McCarthy said, and as I said in a press conference, a fresh sense of the "calling"—the vocation—of the laity is desperately needed today.

I hope I shall not be misunderstood in saying the congress had a "secular agenda" for the exercise of the laity's Christian vocation; that is, a longing for Christian faith and theology to be freshly introduced into the issues of our times through the laity, which has the potential to change society. A secular agenda, of course, simply means an agenda in and for the world and is sufficiently broad to encompass renewal and reform of church institutions. After all, the church is also in the world and if, through its present forms, it is unable to bring the message of love and reconciliation into the world, the laity and the clergy together bear the blame for the failure and must together enliven the institutions—under the guidance of God's Spirit.

I was sorry that the congress schedule could not accommodate a historical survey of those occasions in the American past when the laity took an agenda into the world and not only changed society but also influenced ecclesiastical structures. The modern laity would find encouragement, I believe, in the examples of our ancestors, who joined across denominational lines in great public causes for Christ and social improvement. We may know that the Sunday school was born of lay initiative and was spread across America in the nineteenth century by volunteers dispatched by non-denominational, lay-led organizations. Do we know that the American Home Missionary Society, the American Bible Society, the American Tract Society, and, yes, the American Education Society, an early advocate of theological education for the clergy, emerged in the early eighteen hundreds out of the same strongly lay impetus that undergirded the Sunday school movement? I could hardly overstate the impact those movements had on American society and religion a century or so ago.

Are we aware that it was the Christian laity, women and men, who assumed almost total responsibility for building a network of schools and colleges for the slaves freed in the eighteen sixties? Have we forgotten how the laity dreamed of and built many of this nation's hospitals, orphanages, and community centers? When we read church history, if we read church history, do we miss the pivotal lay involvement in the foreign missionary movement?

But we dare not rest on the laurels of our ancestors and, besides, we need few new colleges or hospitals; we have the Bible Society, the Sunday school, and an ample supply of theological seminaries, and tent meetings seem quaint. Our challenges are different from those of our great and great-great grandparents. We are not called to build new institutions so much as to leaven society, and to do it with as much enthusiasm as was shown by one Stephen Paxson, who established hundreds of Sunday schools along the Illinois frontier in the eighteen forties. For most of us, our frontier, our mission field, our ministry is in that world of home, work, and community affairs where we live every day.

One congress workshop exploring a specific opportunity for lay Christians to be leaven in society and at the same time strengthen the church fellowship was that led by Ron Sunderland, director of the Institute of Religion at Texas Medical Center in Houston. Sunderland is a clergyman, one keenly aware, as many ministers are, of the laity's potential. His workshop was on "The Church as a Caring Community," a title with broader ramifications for a "secular agenda" than one might initially think.

Sunderland has developed a strong argument for a model of greater lay participation in pastoral care, an area of ministry traditionally reserved for ministers as "shepherds" of the flock, including the strays. Pastoral care, he says, is a function of the Christian congregation as a whole and, through individuals, extends into the workaday world. He also finds that certain lay Christians have specific gifts in "pastoring" and should be encouraged and trained to employ those gifts. Sunderland acknowledges possible problems and pitfalls in lay pastoral care, especially if persons who attempt it are inclined to talk when they should listen, but that, of course, is also a pitfall in clerical pastoral care.

Greater lay participation in pastoral care can obviously benefit a congregation by taking pressure off the minister and deepening mutual love and concern. Sunderland has generated enthusiasm and new life within local groups with which he has worked in the area of lay pastoring. But how does his proposal serve "a secular agenda"? Or equip the laity to bring Christian theology and "Christian presence" into society at large?

Any person who learns deeper caring and pastoral skills within a congregation can, of course, translate both the caring and the skills into the plethora of all human relationships. I believe there is an even larger application of the lay pastoring theme and, in this, I am going somewhat beyond what Sunderland says. It is pastoral care, caring for the world in Christ's name, I believe, when lay Christians not only perform acts of love and mercy but also when, by character, word, and example, they challenge impersonal structures, public immorality, social injustice, familial collapse, and all secular explanations of life's meaning. My friend Howard C. Blake has said:

> If humanity is pictured in terms of throngs of people near the edge of a bluff, where many either slip or are pushed over the edge by pressure too strong for them, the Church uses nearly all of its resources to run an ambulance service on the beach below. Is there any way we could build a fence along the cliff above?

I believe the Christian laity offers the most realistic labor force for that fence building; serving humanity spiritually and physically is nothing but pastoral care, spread wide for all God's world.

How long do we endure the culturally induced, secular-supported status quo, which says, "religion is religion and business is business"? How long can we keep enthusiasm for the Gospel of love under a bushel, unless we happen to attend an evangelistic rally where cheers or tears, or both, are in order?

Martha Edens, general director of Church Women United, led a fascinating congress workshop that touched on the issue of the status quo. Her subject was, "The Women's Movement: Creative Action or Reaction?" Something is taking place among many American women, she said. There is a movement for "liberation" from all sorts of stereotypes and social limitations. Churchwomen, said Ms. Edens, must decide how they will respond to the movement.

The laity as a whole and as individuals must decide how we will respond to the movement of Christ's love, which liberates us from sin and selfishness and bids us be agents of love in liberating human bodies, hearts, and minds. Christian love is the leaven for lasting liberation in a society in bondage to a secular status quo.

Abigail McCarthy's congress address, in section B of this chapter, strikes two major notes. First, she discusses the importance of lay ecumenism and of the lay "calling" to Christian vocation in the world. Second, she explores the role of creative artists, especially writers, in helping to form the social community. The second portion beautifully illustrates a committed lay Christian grappling with the contribution of his or her calling to human welfare in this world of hope and despair.

B. CREATIVITY AND COMMUNITY–THE LAY RESPONSIBILITY

Abigail McCarthy

The thought of the people of the evangelical churches moving with all their renewed energy and vitality to join those of us in the more hierarchical churches in the effort to reanimate the world in which we live with the spirit of the Gospel seems the stuff of dreams . . . but the stuff of practical dreams, the kind which bring about real change and movement forward for humanity. The laity of the evangelical churches, it seems to me, comes from a tradition in which the distinction between clergy and lay is not so finely drawn and not so clearly perceived. Hence, they come to social action with no burden of diffidence to shake off and, perhaps, with no doubt of their gifts as lay persons.

My own experience was different as far as my perception of myself as a lay person was concerned. I say it lightly but it comes very near the truth: as a lay woman I could be said to have been on the very lowest rung of the ladder of responsibility—there were bishops, priests, men and women religious (priests, monks, and nuns) lay men—*then* lay women. I must confess that, originally, I didn't object to that hierarchical order. In fact, I thought it was a fine division of labor. There were all those people with special callings—vocations—to take care of things for me—to take care of worship, education, evangelization. I had only to attend, to receive, and to support. It took a long time to grow into a realization that I was called to the priesthood of the people of God—that I, too, had a calling as *a lay person.*

In another way, however, I was closer to the people of the evangelical churches—of all other churches. Before I saw the need for ecumenism—for Christians to be one as Jesus prayed we might be—I was sure that my vision of salvation was the only one. As, I am sure, did they. I am indebted to many people for enlarging my own view but perhaps to no one more than to C. S. Lewis. There is a sermon he preached to graduating students at Cambridge in which he said that the worst temptation they would face in life was to what he called "the inner ring." That inner ring for each of us might be circles of power or of knowledge—it might even be, he said, to a fly fishing club—but always to something which excluded others. Unfortunately, there is a temptation to see in our church an inner ring to which we belong and others do not.

ABANDONING LAY INFERIORITY

That, of course, is one of the first things we have to rid ourselves of. The other is the concept of "lay" as somehow inferior. There can be no doubt that the popular use of the

word "lay" is a pejorative one, or at the very least a conde-
scending one. Once on a shuttle going to New York from
Washington, I saw two very busy-looking young men with
briefcases across the aisle. One of them aid to the other, "Let
me see that prospectus you worked out for the layman.
That's pretty good." The other one laughed and said, "Well,
of course, I left out most of the complexities. After all that's
why they have me as their lawyer."

The secondary definition of "layman" in the American
Heritage Dictionary is: "One who does not have special or
advanced training or skills." The Random House Dictionary
is even worse: "One who is not a clergyman or one who
is not a member of a specified profession; one who is not a
member of the law or medicine," etc. Not, not—*not* something. A negative definition. Not what *is* a layman, what
does he do?

Without going into all of the ramifications of church history, I think we can say that, for one reason or another
throughout history, in one age after another, the fields of
specialized knowledge grew out of the clericature. We tend
to think this is only true of the Middle Ages, when the clergy
were excused from the acts of war and tended to be the only
ones who could read and write and eventually the only ones
who knew the intricacies of law and of healing. But something very like that development occurred in our own American history. Almost all our great academic institutions were
originally training schools for clergymen, and ordained
clergymen tended to head them even after they began to
train for the secular fields. Even the University of Minnesota
in my home state, a land-grant tax-supported institution,
chose, for its first rector, a clergyman.

Until recently, in the institutional church at least, a layman's role has always been a rather passive one. He has been
a consumer of what the clergy prepared for him. When, in
the latter part of the nineteenth century, it seemed possible
that he or she should be sent forth to extend the church, the
thinking was not that the lay missionary had a special or
peculiar role as a lay person but that he was trained as an ex-
tension of the clergy, a propagandist, if you will.

Now, in our own century, we have reached what has been called the age of the laity. The reasons are various. The "de-Christianization" of the West is, of course, one. But just what the laity want to do, exactly what they were called to do, has not been very clearly defined. In one mid-nineteen fifties book on the relationship of the clergy and the laity, the author ends up by saying it's not at all clear what the relationship of the laity to the church should be. However, he found this a cheerful note. Fortunately, he said, "life works out a solution, if only a temporary one, to a host of problems without waiting until theoreticians are ready with their syntheses." With some notable exceptions, the theoreticians and the theologians did a valiant job of catching up with the actual situation of the laity in my own church, in the Decree on the Laity of Vatican II in 1965.

When I first moved into the ecumenical world, I was somewhat surprised to discover that the laity was not all that free in the other churches either. That, in a way, bureaucracies took the place of the hierarchy in many cases, and that initiative and direction came from them rather than from the society of the laity—the grass-roots laity. Mark Gibbs, in the *Audenshaw Documents,* says that the topic of the laity in the institutional churches is a difficult one, "partly because although all the churches from the Roman Catholic to Pentecostal and back again, have worked out a theology of the partnership between clergy and laity, the psychology of the partnership is still very delicate and it is not easy to have an open and helpful discussion on this point. . . . The word laity is not always helpful either—though we have no better one. In some church discussions this word means the people who are loyal churchworkers; while to others it means a great majority of Christian people. . . ."

I drew a great sense of hope, however, from what Mark Gibbs said almost parenthetically. The laity, he said, are naturally ecumenical. "They don't work in Baptist labor unions or in Episcopal stores or live on Presbyterian streets."

THE LAY "CALLING"

The world which is naturally ecumenical, the world of work, is what I want to stress. A great deal of the discussion that swirled about the role of the laity in recent years centered on an apparent dichotomy, which can be stated rather crudely: Does the institutional church and its ministers exist to serve the laity, or does the layman exist to support and help extend the institutional church? Both views assume the world and the world of work are separate and apart. It is only recently that the concept that a layperson might be called to his work—as a member of the clergy is called to his ministry—has taken hold. And yet, only a casual meditation on the parable of the talents would seem to suggest this, as do in different ways the references to the leaven and the mustard seed, the cockles and the wheat growing together until the harvest.

It is dazzling to think that the question of whether laypersons might or might not possess charisms was debated seriously at Vatican II. The decision that he or she indeed might is at least tangential to the concept that a layperson's work might very well be his or her calling. This is not to say that one might have a direct call from God to be a stockbroker but that a talent in brokerage could well indicate that one is to be concerned with the stewardship of money—money that affects the destiny and the happiness of individuals and nations.

I cannot stress enough how different this concept is from the idea that some laypersons are to inject themselves into a certain kind of work because it is a fruitful field for evangelization. One is not sent. One is called, and not for any other reason than that the talent and gifts for that calling are present in the person called. The clearest examples are those of artists and writers. Although there has been a rather generally accepted view that the church is a patron of the arts, the truth is that there has always existed a tension between the arts and the churches. It has been very difficult for the professional churchman to accept art that is not ecclesiastical art, that does not directly serve as an instrument of teaching or evangelization. The examples of churchmen who have forbidden art altogether and have ruled it out as inadmissible in the life of a good Christian are legion. From childhood, I remember reading about Little Elsie Dinsmore. She was a very pious little girl and a very good musician. Her father, who was not anywhere near as pious as Elsie, wanted her to play the piano for some guests on Sunday. She refused. He made her sit on the piano bench and she still refused. She would not profane the Sunday by playing the piano. That story, which I admired very much when I read it, is an indication of the uneasy relationship between the church and the arts at one time or another.

THE CALLING TO THE ARTS

Agatha Christie gives a beautiful reason for what might be called the calling to the arts in her autobiography. She says:

> One does feel proud to belong to the human race when one sees the wonderful things human beings have fashioned with their hands. They have been creators—they must share a little the holiness of the Creator, who made the world and all that was in it, and saw that it was good. But He left more to be made. He left the things to be fashioned by men's hands. He left *them* to fashion them, to follow in his footsteps because they were made in his image, to see what they made, and see that it was good . . .
>
> Men can be evil—more evil than their animal brothers can ever be—but they can also rise to the heavens in the ecstacy of creation.[1]

Dame Agatha, it is important to note, sees creativity in relation to the Creator. The artist, a creature himself naturally, continues the art of creation.

But the function of art is not just to make, to shape, to fashion, to write. It has a public function. Ben Shahn, one of the most thoughtful and one of the most lucid contemporary artists, explains this more clearly than I could hope to do.

[1] Agatha Christie, *An Autobiography* (New York: Dodd, Mead & Co., 1977), p. 443.

He says that the intention of the artist who is a true artist is simply to give shape to content in whatever way it has been given to him to do so. But the reward of the artist's work goes far beyond his intention. Shahn writes:

> The public function of art has always been one of creating a community. That is not necessarily its intention but its result—the religious communities created by one phase of art; the peasant community by another. . . . It is the images we hold in common, the characters of novels and plays, the great buildings, the complex of pictorial images and their meanings, and the symbolized concepts, principles, and great ideas of philosophy and religion that have created the human community. The incidental items of reality remain without value or common recognition until they are symbolized, recreated, and imbued with value. The potato field and the auto repair shop remain without quality or awareness or the sense of community until they are turned into literature by a Faulkner or a Steinbeck or a Thomas Wolfe, or into art by a Van Gogh.[2]

What Shahn is telling us is that community depends on common beliefs and understandings, on a common perception of reality rather than the proximity of living together. Our common beliefs today and our perceptions of reality are more formed by writers than we realize. Therein lies a real problem for the lay Christian who is a writer. Is his writing his apostolate? Does that deform his art?

STORYTELLERS

In a newspaper course developed at the University of California and syndicated in the press, Herbert J. Gans writes that every society has its storyteller. "In the past," he says, "they treated folk tales, folk art, and folk music. Today, they write movie or television scripts and novels, create commercial art, and compose popular ballads and rock and their product is called popular culture." Together with what he calls the "storysellers," they are the makers of the popular culture that affects us all.

[2] Ben Shahn, *The Shape of Content* (Cambridge, Mass.: Harvard University Press, 1957), pp. 130–131.

It is the storytellers who shape us. We tend to live by story. We try to impose order on the formless by means of story. History is nothing but the effort to tell the story of human-kind. Our earliest forebears and the most primitive people tried to explain the mysteries of life and death by story in the process called mythmaking. For us (Christians) there is a basic unity based on story. We are, as we have been called, the People of the Book, and the great majority of us live by a story that has been handed down to us, by acknowledging as Savior he who taught by story. Our minds echo with those stories: "There was a man who went down from Jerusalem to Jericho . . . ," "A sower went out to sow the seeds . . . ," and all the others.

In the nineteenth century, no literate person would say, as I find a lot of literate people saying today, "I never read fiction." Because in the nineteenth century everyone read Scott, Dickens, Balzac, Flaubert, Tolstoy, Dostoevski, Conrad, Austen, George Eliot, Melville, Twain, James. Those names were quite literally household names. In contrast, think how relatively unknown are the names of the critics' choices of the last twenty or thirty years.

Does it matter? Yes, it does. Because, as Lionel Trilling put it in *The Liberal Image,* "The novel is a perpetual quest for reality, the field of its research being always the social world, the material of its analysis is always manners as an indication of man's soul." The real depths of humanity cannot be communicated by abstraction—by philosophy or the social sciences. Human life is so full of hints and contradictions, of currents of feeling, of appearances and what lies behind them, "the look and feel of things, how things are done," to continue quoting Trilling. The English novel penetrated caste and social class and what that meant to people; the French novel layers of the personality, and the great Russian novel, "the ultimate possibilities of the spirit."

I can think of two poignant examples of the novel communicating reality in a way that has an effect on all of us. "Miss Lillian" Carter, the mother of the president, has often told how she turned to books in her effort to give her most promising son a sense of the world beyond the dusty little town of Plains in the Georgia peanut fields. And he has told us that his teacher insisted he read *War and Peace,* Tolstoy's great novel, and that he read it over and over again, and he has told us what that reading meant to him.

The other example is that of the gifted black novelist, Toni Morrison, author of *The Song of Solomon.* With her, contemporary black literature has moved from regional polemic into the great stream of world literature. She has been reproached, she says, for writing fiction in a time when, according to some other black writers, fiction is a luxury. Writing, they say, must be political to be effective. She has this answer, made in an interview reported in the Washington *Star:*

> All good novels are political; all first-rate music is political. It's just in how you approach it. Fiction allows black characters to be seen as individuals, not stereotypes. I have an enormous fondness for Russian peasants because of Dostoyevsky, of Tolstoy. I knew these people when I was little. I read about them. Whatever else is going on politically, I have a human response to those people because I was once inside them.

Fiction, she is saying, allows us to change places, to change skins, to get inside of others as living human beings. And that affects our political and moral development; it affects our relationship to other human beings in the world in which we live. Such art makes us more fully human.

In a time of social change this has more importance than ever. We are endlessly tinkering with our social machinery. We think we know what to do for other people. But not all our moral problems are solved by theories. New wrongs may be generated just as we right old ones. As Trilling put it, there are dangers in our most generous wishes. "Some paradox of our nature leads us when, once we have made our fellow man the object of our enlightened interest, to go on to make them the objects of our pity, then of our wisdom, and ultimately of our coercion."

To counteract this corruption of good intention, we need the moral realism that is the result of the moral imagination—to meet the objects of our interest as other human beings, to "walk in their moccasins." The most effective agent of the moral imagination, Trilling insists, has been the novel of the last two hundred years. It has taught us the extent of human variety. It was the literary form to which the emotions of understanding and forgiveness—forgiveness of ourselves and others—were indigenous. How are we going to recover the work of the imagination, which communicates reality and morality in the true sense of the word—rightness in human relationships? Many of the good novels today give us slices of reality, but we can't enter into them and live as though in another world, as we could in *The Brothers Karamazov*.

LOSS OF IMAGINATION

Part of the problem lies in the larger reading audience today, which is not a compact constituency—an audience on which much of the frame of reference and many nuances are lost. For this audience it seemed necessary to simplify scenes, to ignore texture, and to stick to well-worn themes. It is not that this audience is less intelligent but that it has less in common. On the one hand, this state of affairs is to be deplored for reasons other than the disappearance of the great novel. It has driven much of our aesthetic literature in upon itself. On the other hand, it has raised entertainment literature to new heights of excellence.

This last fact is not necessarily disturbing to writers or readers whose values are shaped by the Judeo-Christian tradition. After all, Dickens and Tolstoy have made good television fare.

C. S. Lewis said that the Christian writer does not feel the same need to be totally creative, to devise new forms, to stem everything out of himself because he knows that no matter what he creates he is only reflecting eternal feeling or eternal wisdom. He or she may have a personal vision, but will have no preference for expressing that personal vision in only one way.

And yet, something is very much wrong with our entertainment literature today. Why is British television so very much better than ours, at least in conveying the variety of human character in the sweep of history? Why does there seem to be only one imagination breaking any new ground in television (whatever one thinks of the value of his work)— that of Norman Lear? Does such a state of affairs not reflect the desperate poverty of creativity?

Agatha Christie wondered in her last writing what had happened to detective fiction. When she started writing, she said, it was so clear that the author would be on the side of the victim, that good should eventually triumph. She said no one could have dreamed there would come a time when crime books would be read for their love of violence, "the taking of sadistic pleasure in brutality for its own sake." One would have thought, wrote Dame Agatha, "the community would rise up in horror against such things." Why doesn't the community rise up? Perhaps because the community fails to realize that it depends on its storytellers for its common vision. "Where there is no vision, the people perish."

The problem is not going to be solved by the layperson who is a writer or artist. It has to be solved by all of us. It is a task for the reader and the viewer. Above all, it is a task for what Herbert Gans called the "storyseller"—of the businessmen whose conglomerates include publishing houses, of the corporations whose advertising departments use works of the imagination solely as a device to aid selling. It is the task, in other words, for laypersons in the world of work.

It is the gift of speech—the wonder of the word—which lifts each of us out of isolation. Through sound and picture and symbol—through the arts—we grow in understanding of truth and beauty, of ourselves, and of others. We need to see that the ability to communicate is a precious gift from God and that with it and through it we build a truly human community.

Chapter Seven

EXPANDING VISION

A. TELEVISION: CAUSE FOR DESPAIR?

Every fall for twenty years critics have wandered through each new commercial television season, calling it a "wasteland," bemoaning the arid themes and shallow morality, and hoping for a better crop of programs next year. Improvements have been so few, so slow, that today many serious people despair of television and have turned their energies from trying to improve it to ways to counteract its influence in the molding of "popular culture." Michael Novak analyzes this despair, saying that television is really not "popular culture" at all because it arises not from the people themselves but is "manufactured by a special class of people educated beyond their ability to understand." Regardless, electronic communication so largely envelops the late twentieth century that we scarcely remember our lives before it. We blame television, fashionably, for all our problems; it becomes our scapegoat, for no doubt it does reflect our materialism, our mindlessness, our personal boredom, our interpersonal deadness, our spiritual poverty.

I think what Novak is digging at in his comment about the "special class" that manufactures television programs is the relational paradox between leader and follower, between "telecaster" and "telereceiver," between the elite far away, who send out program signals, and us, the proletariat who turn the dial. After all, the ratings reflect us—some of us, anyway, and a good many, I suspect. The "special class" provides what "the masses" want, or will accept. And if we will accept schlock, we get it, just as we get unprincipled public officials if we will accept them.

"The media" came up repeatedly in Congress of the Laity keynote addresses and in the ensuing discussions. Malcolm Muggeridge sniped at television, as he frequently does when he has an audience. Abigail McCarthy was less than pleased with the electronic media as "storyseller" in our society. John P. Newport, whose comments are printed later in this chapter, urged church-based studies in media criticism to help Christians understand and respond to a dominant force in modern life. "This country needs a hearing aid," James Reston quipped in a press conference. "The voice of the Lord can't get through the singing commercials."

In sympathy for television people, let me say that, since I appreciate television news with all its inadequacies, and since televised sports come to a Dallas Cowboys fan as a technological grace, and since I actually like some popular shows, I am out of step with parts of the following discussion. I will not say more about my own views here. Let me first act as reporter, then I do have some thoughts of my own on "the media," especially television.

Media as a challenge to the creativity of lay Christians arose at the very outset of the congress in Abigail McCarthy's opening night assertion that writers and other artists are a major source of the common values and visions, the cement, which holds a people together, a nation in community. When that cement is eroded, she said, the social community is threatened, and she was less than sanguine about the prospects of today's media culture supplying values, visions, and cement.

Peter Berger, in the discussion of McCarthy's paper, vigorously disputed the claim that novelists and other artists are singular sources of common values and meanings in society. He also doubted the absence of social cement: "There are millions of people who live together without murdering each other, who respect each other . . . , who have common ambitions, common aspirations and values. That, it seems to me, is what community is about."

Tom Howard disagreed with Berger, saying it seemed to

him that what we have in America today is a "recipe for a dismantled society," with all the shrill clamoring and lack of a common center. Given the immigrant background of most American people, Michael Novak was unconvinced that common values came from reading the same literature, and he had his own particular reason for disparaging of the media as communicator of common values.

NOVAK: What's wrong is that we hardly ever find ourselves reflected in "popular culture," the culture of the media, the culture most of us are forced to live on because there isn't much else that reaches all of us at the same time. When was the last time on television . . . you saw your own neighborhood, or saw your own values lived out. I often want to tell my children, with reference to the celebrity culture which seems so far from everything we stand for, "Celebrities are nice people . . . but I wouldn't want you to marry one." Celebrities of the media represent a world of values foreign to everything we want to stand for. So there's this funny thing. . . . We call the media "popular culture," but it's not from the people. It doesn't well up from the people . . .

MCCARTHY: Actually . . , that's more or less what I meant to say and I don't want to be pushed by Dr. Berger into the "aristocracy of the arts." In fact, that is a problem. Our elite among the artists are having to live almost completely to themselves and that is forcing some very strange forms of art. [In response to Berger] I am not so sure that our community is as cohesive as it was even ten years ago. . . . Research on voting patterns, for example, shows that fewer and fewer Americans feel motivated to enter the political process. That has to mean some decline in our sense of community and our ability to control the world we live in. . . . Many of us don't live by popular culture, but there are many, many people—perhaps the majority of people—who do.

NOVAK: Oh, I don't believe that. . . . I've never met anybody who does—never met a single person who does. . . . I don't hear anything . . . except a kind of contempt for what they see [on television].

. . . .

HOWARD: Michael, how can you say that? It seems to me that of two hundred and eighteen million people probably two hundred and seventeen million are following like sheep what they see on television. I mean . . ., if you stopped twenty people on the street and asked them about some question of human morality, something the human race has agreed on for ten thousand years . . . , most of them would throw up their hands in despair. They wouldn't know.

. . . .

HOWARD: There is certainly no court of appeals whatever in our culture, either for the artist . . . or in public discussion.

NOVAK: One of the virtues of living in a pluralistic society is just that there are many ways you can explore, many ways you can follow.

HOWARD: Is there any example in history of a society like that lasting?

NOVAK: Ours is an experiment, as Lincoln put it. It is an experiment and there is no guarantee that the kind of society in which we now live will be here in thirty years.

America, the experiment—resisting change even as it changes; self-confident and timorous; busy, busy seeking alternatives to any and every possibility; always analyzing and jostling in the lists of disagreement. And it is points in disagreement toward which I am moving.

Do American Christians settle back and let "the media" impose on our culture values and visions foreign to the best in us? Must we be stupefied by the horror movies, the unfunny humor, the commercialized nostalgia and "celebrity culture" of television? Certainly not! Television executives need our protests, and they also need our prayers. But I am not so sure that the manifold criticism heaped upon television these days joins the real issue of "the media" and shallow popular culture. Perhaps I am out of step with much of the criticism of television because I am a grocer.

A modern market manager has a responsibility to stock the good, wholesome foods needed for healthy living, but to stay in business he (or she) must also merchandise what the nutritionist critics call "junk food" because the customers want it (and it is not just a matter of people being hoodwinked by advertisers into thinking they want it). A store whose breakfast cereal section has only oatmeal, because it is "good for you" and no sugar flakes, because they are "not so good for you," will retain few breakfast food customers. I have a suspicion the same principle would apply to television if everything on the tube was suddenly of a type and quality to please that special class whose calling is to criticize television. I have a notion that a steady diet of programs "good for you" in philosophical terms or constantly depicting us as we are in our mundane everydayness would send all of us in search of schlock motion pictures and stage shows.

At any rate, I will take the televised schlock we have—and hope for broader and better fare as cable and other media technologies develop—over any system in which government, or professors of communications, or, worst of all, a panel of media critics dictate contents. And I am not sure we would be better off to put "the people" in charge of programming, as though daily plebicites could decide the schedule for each succeeding night. Frankly, I think we would just get more media sugar flakes than we already have. I am much more comfortable with an arrangement in which persons of both artistic and commercial interests interact in creating television content, and those of us in "the masses" can buy the product or turn off the set. The real problem behind much of the Congress of the Laity discussion of television has as much to do with the exercise of freedom in the relational paradox between "elites" and "masses," between leaders (even phony ones) and followers, as it does with the media itself.

Television and its impact on society is the fruit of seeds planted long before today's popular culture. If television as it exists is more a curse than a blessing, it is not because the networks and the sponsors have benumbed us to our own better welfare. The reason lies far back, with a couple in a garden, a couple we all know, a couple that in freedom swapped what was good for humanity—the companionship of God—for what it thought was good—human autonomy. Whatever else it is, "the media"—and the word in one basic sense means that which transmits or conducts—rather accurately pictures our secular society as it is. Let us not be too quick to condemn a technological system that in large measure merely feeds back to us what we feed into it.

Television is a science; it also qualifies among the arts, and as the most popular medium utilizing artistic creativity it often overshadows the more classical "fine arts." All art provides some degree of entertainment, or delight, but all art has the capacity to bring insight—to be a source of insight. If Abigail McCarthy is right, artists, as distinct from "storysellers," may not be the major suppliers of society's common values today, but across the centuries they still are among the most honored representatives of human creativity. Artists express and whet human aspirations, give voice and form to pain and ecstasy, explore the paradox of hope and the bleakness of despair. Involvement in and encouragement of the arts is, in my estimation, a high calling of the Christian laity today.

We included as many forms of art in the Congress of the Laity as the schedule and space would permit. Music and dance were part of the plenary program. An original ballet based on the novel *St. Francis* by Nikos Kazantzakis was performed by the Valyermo Dancers. We heard Mozart, Gregorian chants, spirituals, and rock music. Before and after sessions, in display areas, corridors, and the lobby of the Regency Hyatt House Hotel, the Lamb's Players of San Diego delighted and probed with mime and puppetry. Painters, lithographers, and photographers were on hand with their works, as was La Liberte with his tapestries.

And we discussed art, the contributions it makes to Christian vision and the contributions the Christian faith has to offer to art. Those issues are treated in John Newport's paper, which follows. Newport, a professor at Rice University in Houston and an author well know among evangelicals, instructively handles the inevitable question of "Christian art" versus "secular art," and proceeds to illumine the edges where faith and art meet.

B. CHRISTIANITY AND THE ARTS

John P. Newport

"What are the most important differences between the 'old days' when you were in college and today?" a student asked me following a university lecture. I mentioned several: one, the development of science and technocracy; another, the phenomenal development of the arts and the media.

By the arts we mean that part of life that expresses itself in the creative, imaginative, and dramatic. This, of course, includes the traditional "fine arts," such as music, painting, literature, sculpture, and architecture. It obviously includes the "lively arts," such as drama and ballet. And in our day it definitely includes the "popular arts," such as movies, television, and radio.

Susan Sontag contends that the new forms of music, literature, drama, painting, and movies are so powerful that they are modifying our consciousness and dominating our lives. Marshall McLuhan says the same thing. He has called our era the "image age." Significant philosophers and psychologists are emphasizing that we are symbol-making creatures in a world of symbols and imagination. Michael Novak, in one of his books, suggests that a person does not live primarily by principles but by stories.

Historically, many conservative religious people, especially Protestants, have been suspicious of the arts. Charles Finney, prominent evangelist of another generation and the first president of Oberlin College, believed all dramatists and actors are "triflers and blasphemers of God." The Puritans were afraid of most art forms. Their church edifices were of-tentimes as austere as barns. Psalms were sung without in-strumental music.

These misgivings are justified to some degree. Is it not true that many artists participate in and dramatize the human rebellion against God? The world of creative imagi-nation, like all of us, is deeply involved in the general cor-ruption of man. Such problems, however, must not keep Christian people from dialogue or conversation with the arts. Dimensions of life as powerful as the arts are ignored to our own loss.

We can pursue the Christian dialogue by asking and seek-ing to answer three questions:

1. What are the contributions that the arts can make to Chris-tianity?
2. What are the possible contributions that the Christian per-spective can make to the arts?
3. What are the limitations of the arts from the Christian perspective?

CONTRIBUTIONS OF THE ARTS

Art is as persistent in history as man himself. At this mo-ment, thousands of people are working with wood or stone, or musical instruments, or brushes and canvas, or film mak-ing or creative television programs. Or, if not creating, we are appreciating other people's creations.

Through the ages, philosophers have attempted to explain man's urge to artistic creativity and his love of the various art forms. We have at least three classic answers to the question of the meaning of art:

——Art is a form of creating, making, or constructing.
——Art affords pleasure, satisfaction, and joy.
——Art is a distinctive form of expression or communication.

These meanings suggest a range of contributions the arts make to Christianity.

Art as Form

The artist teaches us that each person can and should bring form to the chaos of life.

Man is born into a chaos of forms and experiences. To live constructively we must cope with this chaos through some type of orientation.

Artists are more than imitators or expressers of emotion. They also construct material into structured form. An art form is fundamentally a structure with its own independent existence and value. From one perspective, an artist is a person who sees chaos, but in some way makes sense out of it. The ways in which artists set forth their apprehensions of reality are extremely varied. Much of art is given over to the celebration of the nature of things. The realist tradition, exemplified by Andrew Wyeth, continues. Other artists do not so much see and analyze as feel and react. Many modern visual artists reflect the breakup, fragmentation, and flux of our times. From a more positive perspective, artists reflect the new pluralism of our society.

The artist also helps us to renew life. Man needs a world that is constantly renewed, for yesterday's wonderful tends to become today's commonplace. In the words of Whitehead, "The freshness of being evaporates under mere repetition." Creativity becomes an endless process because renewal is a necessity of the nature of man.

The Christian profits from seeing life as a work of art. He learns from realism, expressionism, and abstractions. He seeks to understand the forces that cause breakup and fragmentation. In addition, the arts remind him anew of those principles and resources in his faith that can bring symmetry, balance, proportion, and constant freshness and renewal.

Art as Pleasure

Art can remind the Christian of the resources for sheer pleasure in the Christian drama.

In many Christian circles it seems to be sinful to exhibit too much satisfaction and happiness and joy. Some say,

"How can Christians be happy and enjoy life in a world of spiritual and physical need?"

The importance of pleasure and play as necessary ingredients of a balanced life has long been recognized. The ancient Roman rulers gave the people circuses and gladiator shows to release pent-up pressures and to lessen life's burdens. Communist societies sponsor mass sports, pleasure palaces, and artistic festivals. The medieval church gave the people a Mardi Gras festival of excesses as a prelude to the demands of the Lenten period. The Church allowed the Feast of Fools, the Feast of Asses, and Easter laughter.

And in recent years the artistic world has been confronting us with a new aesthetics. Susan Sontag, in her book *Against Interpretation,* writes, "Transparence is the highest, most liberating value in art today. Transparence means experiencing the luminousness of the thing in itself, of things being what they are." The new aesthetics wants to leave the categories of meaning and hope to others. The artist says, "I want to put an emphasis on the sensuous surface and sound of things: the fantastic colors of psychedelic experience, the fresh voices of electronic music and light shows."

Christians have problems with this perspective if the sensual and psychedelic is all there is to art. But the artist's emphasis on the inherent worth of nonpragmatic pleasure and joy has helped Christians to examine or reexamine their own resources in that regard. Theologian Karl Rahner suggests that God created the world as a playground for his pleasure. The purpose of man's creation is to glorify God and to enjoy him forever. It was God's good pleasure for his Son to become man to redeem and restore us to his favor and fellowship. Since the Cross and Easter, Christians have special reasons for joy and celebration. Even the Last Great Day is seen not just as escape or payday but as a time of joy and fulfillment.

The Christian community ideally is a place of joy, happiness, and celebration as well as a place for education and social-ethical activities. Within the Christian perspective there is a legitimate place for leisure, relaxation, and entertainment. We can even study theology and the Bible out of curiosity and joy in the subject matter. Theology at its heart is an art.

Worship itself should have spontaneity and creativity within biblical limits. The medium is the message at least in a partial way. The religious dance has come back into its own in many churches. What some call the extremism of charismatic churches can be explained in part as a reaction to the coldness, rigidity, and formalism of many middle-class churches.

Man is not just what he produces. The Christian person finds his deepest sense of worth in the fact that God loves him and Christ has died for him. He is accepted and loved as he is. The Christian can thus be joyful. His religion is not just an opiate to compensate for unbearable conditions. Christians anticipate the joy of heaven, but we can also have joy and festivity now.

Art as Rest

The arts can bring rest to life. This is an idea closely related to the biblical idea of the quiet of the Sabbath. All work, manual or mental, tends to produce a hardness and tension in life. As we move further into the technological age, we feel in a new way the necessity of art in our lives. At least some types of art can spiritualize the physical and sensualize the spiritual.

Art forms seem especially helpful to urban people who do not have immediate touch with nature. Crowds throng urban museums on Sunday afternoons. When business leaders of Seattle, Washington, were criticized for their city's relative lack of museums and art opportunities compared to Eastern cities, they responded by pointing out Seattle's proximity to the beauties of nature.

Art and Ultimate Questions

The arts help to raise the ultimate questions to which the biblical faith speaks. In a secular world, artists force people to stop and ask "Who am I, what is my destiny, what is my purpose?" Denis De Rougemont suggests that art forms are "calculated traps to force us to meditate." Nathan Scott sees art forms, especially literature, asking the questions of human existence that the Christian faith answers. Novelists and dramatists often force us to face such problems as guilt (Camus, *The Fall, The Plague*), isolation (Kafka, *The Castle*), original sin (William Golding, *The Lord of the Flies*), and the meaning of success (Arthur Miller, *The Death of a Salesman*).

Donald J. Drew, in *Images of Man*, suggests that many contemporary films reveal man's search for meaning and identity. Variants of Descartes' "I think, therefore I am" are stated. "I copulate, therefore I am" is the view affirmed in *Last Tango in Paris*. In many films, according to Drew, pornography is elevated to idolatry. What is new in pornography is that it promises to provide meaning and purpose in life. Other variations are "I trip [drugs], therefore I am," "I work, therefore I am," and "I play, therefore I am."

In some cases, the arts spell out in dramatic fashion the full implications of what it means to live in a world without God. If a young person wants to know the implications of atheism let him study Jean-Paul Sartre's *No Exit* or *Nausea* with their statement, "Hell is other people."

The artists give access to the concerns and feelings of a culture a generation ahead of more abstract and speculative thinkers. Amos Wilder contends that Christianity can learn from the dynamic mythology of each age the emphases of the Christian message that are most needed. In the Victorian era of nineteenth-century Europe and America, for example, practically everyone accepted the fact that man would live on either in heaven or hell. The contemporary artists have made us realize that another basic question is now being raised. The Theatre of the Absurd, for example, asks if life has any meaning—now or ever.

Art Sifts Tradition

Art forms, especially literature and drama, are oftentimes effective instruments to point out how Christian practice is a distortion of the ideal or is inconsistent with the avowed faith. Art forms help sift traditions and purify sacred arts. They awaken churches to the issues of good and evil.

Using satire and irony, the dismal asceticism and cult of

ugliness in some religious circles are exposed. In other cases, the social immoralities of caste and irresponsible wealth, as sanctioned by religion, are held up for examination. Who can forget Sinclair Lewis's exposure of fraud in evangelism in *Elmer Gantry?*

It's true that modern agnostic writers often ridicule restricted views that prophetic religious leaders themselves are opposing. While it is also true that some attacks on Christian patterns of life may be rooted in positivist, hedonist, or Marxist presuppositions, many artistic indictments direct themselves not at the Christian faith itself but at its distortions and betrayals. William Faulkner, for example, sees and exposes some of these distortions. With a gift for satire and the grotesque, Faulkner scrutinizes the practices of fossilized religion. The whole fable of Faulkner's *The Sound and the Fury* points toward a healthful order of values that has been violated.

The arts can help in the communication of the Christian message. Christian faith involves more than mental assent to an intellectual body of doctrine. It is centered around a person, Jesus Christ. Relationship to God in Christ involves the emotions and will as well as the mind. Artists who deal in symbols can teach Christians a great deal about dynamic, concrete, and symbolic communication.

Drama, by using conflict, can arouse and provoke an audience at deep emotional levels. Sören Kierkegaard, the nineteenth-century Christian literary artist, used a variety of indirect literary devices, such as paradox, irony, and dialectic to stir, provoke, and arouse his readers. Poet T. S. Eliot used dramatic conflict in *The Cocktail Party* to help secular audiences discover for themselves their emptiness and need of spiritual help. In *The Sound and the Fury,* Faulkner presents some of the positive resources of the Christian faith. He does this in the last section, in the account of the church service, and of the sermon of the black preacher. Faulkner sets forth the life-giving mystery and the perennial vigor of the Christian faith among the poor in spirit, in contrast to the way religion is used by some of the more affluent whites.

Other art forms afford significant communications resources. The visual arts can communicate in ways inaccessible to the purely verbal arts. Music has great emotional power. No sermon or doctrinal presentation can portray the sorrow and joy of the Crucifixion and Resurrection as well as music. The worship of many evangelical churches lacks an authentic emotional element.

Evangelical groups have come to power and influence in the nonestablished religious pattern of American life. There is a correlative responsibility for these groups to understand and create new and constructive art forms to patronize arts of quality and creativity. In times past, the free church evangelical groups have been aesthetically mediocre. They have had to depend heavily on Roman Catholic and Anglican artists. The power and value of the arts call for conservative Christian people to give up their fear of the artistic, to go beyond nineteenth-century styles and sentimentalism.

Art and the Bible

The arts can help the Christian community to understand and interpret the Bible in a more adequate way. In fact, the Bible's meaning and purpose can be impaired if it is mechanically literalized or if the dramatic parts are not taken seriously. Bible stories and doctrines are not to be abandoned. Rather, they should be understood and interpreted in ways that escape outworn clichés and secondhand recitations. Martin Luther urged the young people of his time to study literature, drama, and poetry as an aid to a proper understanding of the Bible.

E. H. Peterson contends that failure to see the Book of Revelation as a literary whole has resulted in a literalistic distortion of the book. Revelation, Peterson says, is not a book to be put into scientific schemes and charts. We should not historicize every detail. We would learn to appreciate it as an inspired book of artistic images and aesthetic visions full of wonder, beauty, truth, and hope. Great universal principles and helpful insights are embedded in these visions. They become clear as we study this book as a whole, and in the light of its literary and historical background. For example, behind the vision of Christ coming on a white horse in Revelation 19, we catch the significant truth that there will be ultimate victory, that Christ's presence in power will inaugurate the last great stage of his kingdom. To see the biblical books as literature does not contradict the idea that the literary visions are inseparably connected with God's actions in history in the past and his promised actions in the future.

Bruce Lockerbie is among those who say that the early chapters of Genesis constitute a clear example of an inspired mind using figurative and poetic language in an artistic way. Genesis, says Lockerbie, is not meant to be a technical book of science. The writer uses artistic parallelism like an artist working on a great mural. Randolph Klassen adds that Genesis 1 was intended by the Spirit of God to be read or sung by believers in adoring tribute to the wonderful creator. To force it into categories of scientific precision is like trying to justify Rembrandt's *Night Watch* by a chemical analysis of the oil paint.

Artists can also help us appreciate the beauty of the Song of Solomon, the poetry of the prophets, and the magnificence of Ezekiel's visions. And I wonder if we have fully appreciated the drama of Job and the satire of Jonah. In the New Testament we are coming to appreciate even more the drama of Mark and the artistry of John's gospel. . . . The Bible is faithful to events but it is given to us in dramatic form so that its message can reach a wide audience and convey an indelible impression.

If art forms are so important, Christians should encourage art and media education. Art is both subjective and objective, but artistic perception and ability can be developed. In painting we can learn of color, form, and balance. Art appreciation is highly individualistic, yet there are canons and rules of meaning, truth, and greatness.

CONTRIBUTIONS TO THE ARTS

What are the possible contributions that the Christian perspective can make to the arts?

Theological Backdrop

Christianity can provide a dynamic theological and philosophical backdrop for artistic creations.

The Christian perspective affirms creation, a linear and forward-looking view of history, and man made in God's image with freedom. It further teaches that man used his freedom to rebel. Without destroying or overriding freedom, there is a description of God's redemptive movement in history involving the Hebrew nation, the Incarnation and the Christian community; there is a personal and cosmic purpose.

This Christian view helps to explain man's urge to create. God is the supreme artist and creator. In a mysterious way, man retains some of God's image despite the fall. Man is a subcreator under God. Is it any wonder that man has a creative impulse? We are to engage in a positive calling to create on a finite level as God creates on an infinite level.

Christian theologians would grant with Kant that disinterested aesthetic pleasure has importance. There is a proper place for sensory pleasures in shapes, colors and textures. In the Song of Songs (4:1–7) the bridegroom dwells with relish on the bride's beauties. Behind the surface of the Christian drama, however, is metaphysical depth and underlying purpose. Even that which appears to be ugly can be transformed into beauty. For example, from the eternal perspective, there is beauty in Jesus on the Cross; in fact, the Cross is a way of spiritual accomplishment and a prelude to the Resurrection.

The Christian is convinced that profound artistic life will wither in societies with a reduced spiritual and metaphysical depth. Art tends to degenerate to mere cleverness and virtuosity, which cannot move the heart. Grand passions originate from spiritual depth and tensions.

Amos Wilder, who is both a literary critic and a biblical scholar, finds in the Bible a foundation and a model for contemporary literature. Good literature in any generation could well emulate such qualities as biblical realism and the nonaristocratic level of the biblical narrative and personalities. An additional quality found in the Bible is holism, or an overarching world plot with a beginning and fulfillment. The Bible also demonstrates an ability to portray human experience in concrete language. Noteworthy in the Bible is its oral background, depth of motive, prominence of the verb, and sensuous vocabulary. Out of these biblical features, Wilder singles out three in particular which help in assessing modern narratives: the ability to hold the reader's attention, the holism of the story, and the inclusion of the dramas of the heart.

The Christian view accepts the fact that by common grace all men have spiritual longings and create religious myths. There must be some truth in the Jungian view that identifies these "archtypes" as fundamental and universal symbolic patterns. Religious phenomenologists, such as Mircea Eliade, have discovered these motifs in both primitive and sophisticated societies. Such images as the creation, the fall, the hero figure, the dying and rising god, slaying of monsters, incarnation, and yearning for paradise, rebirth and resurrection are in all men's mythic consciousness.

We Christians believe that in the biblical world view these mystical longings and images are crystallized, historicized, and fulfilled. Around Christ these images are reconstituted in a powerful way as the Incarnation, the Messiah, the New Covenant, the Word, the Cross and the Kingdom. These master images as transformed by Christ and the Bible afford artists dynamic and balanced themes of universal interest and power.

Although there are relatively few explicit Christian artists of prominence, there are some who set forth facets of the biblical perspective in implicit or veiled terms. Within the last two decades, one can think of Graham Greene, T. S. Eliot and Christopher Fry. More explicit writers and dramatists include Charles Williams, Alan Paton, C. S. Lewis, François Mauriac, Dorothy Sayers, Philip Turner, and Flannery O'Connor.

Rigorous Evaluation

The arts can profit from the challenge of rigorous Christian evaluation and discrimination.

Christians will grant the importance of form as opposed to content in a work of art. A film, for example, is to be assessed on the quality of its script, casting, action, location, camera work, color, sound, and editing. Stylistic analysis is important. The Christian says, however, that art forms do reflect world visions or views. Wilder suggests that all imaginative creations offer views of reality. For a Christian, in addition to its form, a film can also be assessed on the relative truth or falsity of its overall theological or philosophical statement. More than the aesthetic experience is involved; not art for art's sake. There is no neutral film, painting, or novel.

Unlike Matthew Arnold, Christians do not tend to see artists as priests and art galleries as worship centers. Artists, it is true, have power; therefore, their views are especially important. Their world views need to be analyzed and their implications brought out in the open—what Wilder calls a "testing of the spirits."

Both the professional theologian, the Christian leader, and the Christian layperson feel an obligation to evaluate art forms in terms of biblical criteria. Hopefully, it will be an informed evaluation. Christians should view films, for example, with a solid grasp of who man is and what truth is. Today, as in the biblical times, the Christian community is confronted with ambiguous cults of ecstasy, eros, and the esoteric.

James Wall, a prominent Christian editor (of the *Christian Century*), contends that increasingly the mass media provide the myths, symbols, and images for the majority of American people. These myths tell us who we are and what we can do. They tell us who has power and what is right and permissible. (In all fairness, it should be noted that the mass media are different from other art forms in terms of their group creation and mass appeal.)

The media thus provide a kind of religious framework.

They provide us with a belief and value system. They express the things that we uncritically assume as given in our lives. For example, there is a tendency in the mass media to tell us that we are basically good and that material happiness is the chief end of life. Authentic sexuality is often transformed into "sex appeal," and the value of self-respect into pride. Authentic will-to-live is made into will-to-power. Recreation is changed into competition. Rest is made into escape. These media myths reach us less at the intellectual level than at the level of dream and fantasy. This image-symbol-subconscious level is obviously more powerful than the intellectual level.

Marshall McLuhan calls for some groups to create an antienvironment. He thinks the artists can do this work. But Robert Bellah in *The Broken Covenant* calls for the urgency of the perspective supplied by religion. Many of the media myths are obviously contrary to the historic Christian ideals. The arts and America can profit if Christian leaders revive in Christian people the ability to identify myths and evaluate them from a biblical perspective. Unfortunately, the media reflect the greed and weaknesses of Christian people far more than we care to admit.

Most cultural analysts say that the place to counteract these myths is where people meet face-to-face in small groups. This is precisely where the Christian churches have strength. Here is where media and art evaluation can and must take place.

Christian people live by hope. They know that men and societies are in Adam. They know that the mass media reflect this Adamic way. Christian people affirm, however, that they have been given a vision. Any constructive help will take clear thinking, hard work, and divine resources. It is an exciting challenge. Alvin Toffler, of *Future Shock* fame, says that Americans are starving for positive images of the future. Nathan Scott suggests that it is time for the realistic and revelatory "art of the fall" to give way to that to which it is always pointing, the "art of redemption." The Christian should stand ready to share the positive images he has found in the Christian vision.

LIMITATIONS OF ART

What are the limitations of the arts from the Christian perspective?

Faith More Than Aesthetics

Art forms may symbolize and suggest spiritual truth, but from the Christian perspective art forms have limitations as far as revealing it goes. Christianity is more than art. It is redemptive, ethical, and practical as well as aesthetic. Symbols should not be converted from means of communication into false centers of worship. In fact, art presents the constant temptation to identify the Holy God of the universe with the beautiful.

According to Michael Novak, the aim of the aesthetic conscience is to create of the feelings a work of harmony, balance, and pleasure. In its higher ranges, the aesthetic conscience pursues beauty at any cost, independent of honesty, courage, freedom, community, and other human values. It prefers form, sweetness, and ecstasy. In its lower forms, the aesthetic conscience is the pursuit of novelty, sensation, adjustment.

It is more comfortable to live with an art form than with the Holy God of the universe. Many sophisticated people interested in the arts are not prophetic or ethically concerned. Some artistic types, like many of us, are unethical when it comes to something that will affect their own private economic or personal interest. Some people in America who are interested in the arts are not interested in an authentic religion that forces them to face the ethical and practical challenge of the God of Jesus Christ.

Idolatry

The exaltation of artistic genius sometimes leads to godlessness. For Schelling, the German philosopher, artistic genius was almost identical with God. In fact, the more creative an artist, the more he is tempted to confuse himself with God. Historian Jarslov Pelikan suggests that Richard Wagner came close to this position. Friedrich Nietzsche, more profoundly than anyone in his time, attempted to find God in the subtle stirrings of the beautiful. Despair and madness finally came when Nietzsche realized that the authentic God refuses to be taken captive—even by the beautiful.

For the Christian, in the area of the arts and the media, there is danger lurking in the shadows. But there is also the possibility of a positive relationship.

Christianity should seek to understand the nature and purposes of art. It should recognize artistic values and contributions. It should not seek to suppress authentic art and legitimate artistic freedom. Art forms can be glorious and fruitful servants. At the heart of the Christian vision, however, is a realization that even art cannot be allowed to be the master.

A prominent literary figure tells of two Englishmen standing on the shores of the Atlantic getting ready to sail to a distant land. One is a symbolic artist and the other a symbolic Christian.

The symbolic artist says, "Let us sail, let us experience the wild blue yonder; let us take risks; let us live sensuously and dangerously."

The symbolic Christian responds, "I want to sail. I am adventurous too. I want to experience life in its fullness. But I want to take my map. This map is composed of the experiences of men who have safely sailed the seas before. It has guidelines prepared by the master pilot."

Christians would agree that life should be dramatic and exciting. Life should be explored in its depth and heighth and breadth, but there are guidelines for the Christian, which he believes reflect revealed insights and sources of power and perspective. He will sail with these guidelines in hand and heart.

Christians need the arts; Christian people also affirm the importance of their ancient yet always contemporary map for the exciting journey of the creative life.

C.   ART AND THE
"CORPORATE HONCHO"

Midway in the panel discussion following Newport's address, Gary Demarest, panel moderator, received from the audience and read this question: "How does a corporate honcho fit whatever it is you're talking about into his marriage, his office, his relationship with his pimply teen-age son who never sees him? How does art, creativity, etcetera, minister to and help me to understand the meaning of my faith?"

It was a question! The previous conversation had touched on the use of artistic forms in expressing the Christian message, on symbolic language, the increasing interest in art among evangelical Protestants, and on the problems of television. Just how does art minister to and help a "corporate honcho" understand faith in his everyday world?

Peter Berger linked his personal frustrations with those of the questioner. "I know very little about the arts and if that's what we're going to talk about, I'm going to be respectfully silent," he said. But like any good professor, he had one observation, and it was very helpful. If art is anything, Berger said, it is a particular way of dealing with reality and transforming reality, yet not transforming it. "It's the same world, the same world that was there all the time, yet somehow it is transformed," he remarked, continuing:

BERGER: That method strikes me as a very profound one if we are to talk about the relationship of Christian faith to the various aspects of life. . . . It is an article of Christian faith that transformations are indeed possible. It's somewhere between magic, which is belief that one can change the world completely, and resignation that nothing can be done about reality. This is something, it seems to me, that links the frustrations and, sometimes, agonies of personal life, and the social realities. A lot of the things referred to by the "corporate honcho," things that happen to our children or to us, we cannot fundamentally change, cannot magically transform them, yet somehow we are able, as Christians, to take these realities and transform them into something hopeful and redemptive. This applies also to how we look at America, at social realities, the historical and political processes we cannot magically transform and about which we can often be very pessimistic. And yet, there is a hope; there is the possibility of transformation.

NEWPORT: It seems to me we are going to have to face the reality of the power of the arts—especially the power of the media. In terms of marriage and corporate business life, the churches must come to grips with the images being portrayed in the popular media. . . . We need to use media as occasion for dialogue on our positive Christian view on marriage, on sexuality, on purpose for the child, and for the home. . . . Our daughter wanted to see Tennessee Williams's *Baby Doll*. We let her go, then had a long talk with her on Williams's Social Darwinism. We found this to be a very helpful approach, because one of the biggest problems of teaching, of communicating, is getting peoples' interest aroused. If they have just seen some movie or some television program, everybody has to see it so they can talk about it in the office; this can be used as occasion for dialogue. We have . . . to take advantage of all this world in which we live. We can't stop it . . . so we just have to criticize and evaluate and use it.

HOWARD: . . . An abyss seems to exist between the daily, ordinary workday world . . . and the vacuum-packed artistic world. . . . Yet the artist, the poet, the dramatist, the playwright . . . is never working with any material other than the stuff of ordinariness. . . . And it's according to how he uses the stuff of ordinary life that decides whether he's a put-on or a prophet. . . . Andy Warhol paints a Brillo box or a Campbell's Soup can and makes a million dollars for doing it. Why? Because he is, in effect, unfurling a flag and saying, "Okay, America, this is what it has come to. You're down to the A&P—there's the essence of your life." Which is fine with me, but the dimension of glory and mystery has gone out. The artist of the twelfth century could paint an Anuniciation. Why? Because he believed the flesh of the Virgin Mary represented us all and that we have been hailed by the divine glory. . . . Do we or do we not believe today that the human race has been hailed by divine glory?

. . . .

NEWPORT: . . . I think one of the responsibilities of the church is to encourage art education, media education . . . for most of our people do not understand what the artists are all about. . . . In my own particular life, if I had not had some people who helped me in understanding, I would be a greatly impoverished person. . . . We and the churches need to undergird and to encourage the arts in communities.

NOVAK: There's a strong reason why we need to learn such things. We're getting images all the time telling us that if we use a certain product everything goes well. If you brush with the right toothpaste you get the job, you get the date, or whatever . . . or use a special shampoo and you discover the true woman within you. . . . When we preach the gospel in this context, it comes out like, "Turn to Jesus and get this miraculous success." . . . Christianity comes out like a toothpaste, like hair rinse. . . .

The use of television in communicating the Christian gospel was discussed briefly early in the panel. Newport volunteered that he is personally uneasy with the new national religious networks. He said:

These are worrying me because, I think, some of the things they teach will play right in with some of the secular presuppositions that should be questioned. . . . Some are indirectly monetary. I was on one of the national charismatic networks by accident and was just overwhelmed by some of the questions people called in from all over the nation. Some of the presuppositions evident in their questions just overwhelmed me. I didn't know what to say. Here I was, supposed to be a guest on the program, and I couldn't accept the presuppositions of the questions. So I feel we have it from both angles now. The new charismatic networks are becoming tremendously powerful politically, and many of the politicians are recognizing it. They are going to be a great political element in the future. We have an interesting thing. We, as Christians, are going to have to constantly watch the "Godhucksters" and we're going to have to constantly watch the secular media. . . . The Christian way is very difficult and subtle.

I would like to see Newport's final comment printed on posters and distributed worldwide: "The Christian way is very difficult and subtle."

Chapter Eight

THE SEARCH FOR
THE COMMON GOOD

A. AMERICA AND MORALITY

James Reston provided one of the most quotable and, by the
press, one of the most quoted statements at the Congress of
the Laity. America is a "moral pigsty," said the *New York
Times* columnist. The phrase carries its own nuances both for
closer scrutiny of the moral condition and for measures toward improvement, and it contributed a graphic metaphor
to the congress dialogue. I like the dramatic description, but
in the conversation following Reston's speech, Peter Berger
thought "pigsty" too pungent. Michael Novak found a paradox in the emphasis on "moral crisis" at a time when, it
seems to him, "we are drowning in morality," at least in the
language of morality: unprecedented, almost obsessive, public attention to what is "good" and "bad" for health, causes of
all sorts cast in terms of absolute "right" and "wrong"; and
politicians on all sides choosing their vocabularies from the
list under "virtue" in *Roget's Thesaurus.*

Take or leave the "pigsty" metaphor and, despite the language of morality bandied about today, America, as Berger
said, is no "moral wonderland." Residues and potentials for
decency, yes, we have both, but there is something grotesque
in the way we cleave to Malcolm Muggeridge's American
four: food, drugs, beauty, and gas, which through over-in-
dulgence anesthetize the senses we need for a cohesive, creative, and moral society. Values too often float like leaves on
a pond, tossed by the latest wave or gust of wind. Women

are reduced to sex objects and men are too weak or too blind to see what they are doing. Bureaucracy oppresses the tax-payers, depersonalizes the welfare recipients, and numbers each of us for easy reference. The poverty we permit, the in-justices we condone, the public indifference we cultivate, and the private behavior we glorify make sport of our moral pretensions, as individuals and as a people.

Reston argues (Section B of this chapter) that neglect of individual duty is a primary cause of our society's moral ca-lamity. Refuting the dictum, "the people have no influence," he urges the connecting of personal and national morality. His point is as straightforward as a freshman civics lesson and may seem simplistic to some but I personally wish all Americans would hear and heed the lesson.

Mike Novak sees irony in talk of a moral crisis when the language of morality is pervasive. I see tragedy in our em-phasis on society's responsibility to persons at a time when personal responsibility to society seems to be going out of date. Strange and marvelous things have happened in America across the past two decades. Marvelous, to me, is the dawning truth that all political and economic struc-tures—indeed, all social structures—must be open and re-sponsive to all citizens. Yet somehow, strange to me, al-though perhaps not surprising, the more the structures of government, education, business, or whatever are changed to afford greater opportunity, service, and accountability to people, the less concern we, the people, have for the very in-stitutions of which we expect so much. The more we expect of government in guaranteeing our rights, in protecting us from harmful chemicals, in regulating business ethics, and in assuring full employment, the more cynical of government we become. The more participation we have in community processes, the more we stay away from the polls. In an era of unparalleled demands on social institutions, we turn to a "do your own thing" psychology, which, in politics, becomes spe-cial-interest lobbying and, in religion, Christianity anyway, tends toward a "me and Jesus" mentality, with no apparent sense of responsibility for the church as it gives historical and temporal expression to a very social faith. Vietnam, the political assassinations of the nineteen sixties and Watergate damaged our national psyche—eroded our confidence and besmirched our national self-esteem, or so it seems. But I am unable to believe we help the situation by lapsing into the "Me" generation's fierce privitism, and that is why I wish every American would hear and heed Reston's civics lessons, his homily on a basic American principle.

A question that fell between the cracks in the post-Reston speech discussion is worth pursuit here. Gary Demarest wondered why the contemporary "evangelical awakening," the emphasis on being "born again," seems to be having little effect on culture and on our social structures. "That is unlike every great evangelical awakening in the past," he said. His question and his observation are on target. Perhaps some of us are too impatient, yet I do wonder if the present "awakening" will have social implications of the kind accompanying the Second Great Awakening of the early nineteenth century. Or maybe the "awakening" today is a figment of the media's imagination? If on the personal level it is real, then I believe we of the evangelical household will be led by God from a stage one, "born again" experience, to a stage two, a socially and relationally engaged faith.

If personal and national morality are to be connected, Reston says, the impetus will likely come from a "moral remnant." "Remnant"—there is a word to gladden the hearts of students of the Bible. How often the Hebrew prophets of the Old Testament harken to a remnant of the people as the embodiment of fidelity, the bearer of hope. I am convinced that the Christian laity of North America can be a moral remnant, a preserving salty tang, in the linking of personal and national, or social, morality. I may be a dreamer, but I dare think we can make a difference in both the moral attitude and behavior of this society, that we can offer moral leavening through a new quality in our leadership. Now I know one school of thought today abhors the words "leader" and "leadership." To project teachers, lawyers, scientists, or even ministers as examples is, in this school, elitist, propagandistic, or worse, disrespectful of our God-given right to follow our own drummer. Poppycock. Glance at the "ce-

lebrity culture" (the Novak term) and tell me we have ma-
tured beyond the need for leadership. When actors, beauty
queens, television announcers, and baseball players draw
crowds just for showing up "in person," when Congress is
picketed by a crowd demanding Elvis Presley's birthday as a
national holiday, when "well known for being well known"
depicts our obsession with fame, then I know people are
casting about for leaders.

There is, of course, a big, big difference between being a
media celebrity and an examplary lay Christian in everyday
work and civic affairs. A hundred to one, no promoter will
bring out a series of posters highlighting the Ipana smiles of
Christian engineers or the "brain appeal" of Christian librar-
ians. (The popular attention engendered by the recent celebrity conversions—I should say the conversions of the celebrated—is a small clue to our social search for a belief in
transformation.) Christian motivation in acting as moral
leaven is quite different from promotion or publicity. It calls
attention not to the importance of the individual, but, as the
individual loses his life to find it, to the focus of our faith
expressed in appropriate love, bit by bit transforming the
moral climate.

I am not saying that Christian laity laboring on the moral
front should presume the goal is to transform our society
into a latter-day version of the Hebrew theocracy or of the
New England Puritan commonwealth. Our society is and
must continue to be pluralistic. I am uncertain which of several definitions of pluralism is best applied to our society,
but I am reasonably sure pluralism is neither of two things.
First, it is not mere toleration of minority groups and opin-
ions by a majority, be that majority racial, ethnic, cultural, or
religious (or possibly irreligious). Second, it is not an amalga-
mation of all distinctions, a boiling down of differences into
some universally thin cultural soup. I like what Bill Lawson,
black pastor and instructor at the University of Houston,
said in a Congress of the Laity workshop on race relations
and urban needs. "Pluralism," he said, "is people learning to
live in juxtaposition to people without suppressing one another." Pluralism means black Americans persuaded to

Islam neither derive their rights from white Christian sufferance nor are they under obligation to look and think like Christians except when they are in their home or mosque. Similarly Christians of whatever race or denomination have no right to force their theology and morality upon the whole of the culture and yet, at the same time, neither are they required to pretend their religion is synonymous with humanitarian good will.

Not infrequently, these days, evangelicals are given to believe it is somehow un-American to evangelize—that words and actions intended to share the faith and increase the community of faith violate the spirit of the First Amendment, twisted around to guarantee only the freedom *not* to have religion. What nonsense. What is to be avoided is arm twisting, psychologically insensitive evangelism. Christianity stripped of its particularity in Christ is not Christianity at all. It is a mystery to me how the secular defenders of pluralism rise to do battle for the right of any Hindu guru, syncretistic group or self-styled messianic movement to aggressively make converts, maybe to sell spirituality, and how those same keepers of pluralism snarl at the mention of Christian evangelism. There is something to be said for special vigilance in protecting the religious rights of small groups, and something also to be said for the right of a majority faith to evangelize so long as it does not suppress or oppress other religious expressions.

Pluralism, as I see it, is the politically appropriate expression of love. Freedom inheres in love, originating in God who did not make us robots. Since there is no freedom without diversity, our challenge is to recognize the coexistence of unity and diversity. The glory of America, and of the vision of democracy that has emerged in the Judeo-Christian heritage, is its commitment to government by talk, not by force: to talk it out, to argue, debate, negotiate—to honor both unity and diversity. It is for this reason that press and media freedom, along with liberty of individual expression, are so crucial in a democracy, and, conversely, as Solzhenitsyn said in his famous Harvard speech in June 1978, why it is so perilous when unfaddish or unpopular points of view cannot be

[125]

heard effectively. The great thing about a pluralistic society is that gay liberationists and Anita Bryant can both "have at it" in the public forum.

"Differences among religions are deeply significant," says the Hartford Appeal, issued in January 1975, by a diverse group of Protestant, Roman Catholic, and Eastern Orthodox theologians. Religious differences remain perennially significant; they matter, and are to be respected in a pluralistic society, just as the freedom to be different must be guaranteed. Pluralism need not dilute. It evokes the strengths of particular groups in the search for the common good, and Christians have enormous (perhaps crucial) contributions to make to public and national moral renewal. After all, the Judeo-Christian tradition is the major—though not the sole—source of founding principles still basic to our society.

Within the context of American pluralism, how does the Christian laity become moral leaven, bring together personal and national morality along the edges where hope struggles with despair? This is not the place for a long treatment of how faith is put into practice but I do want to suggest a style of lay moral engagement in the world adapted from a workshop at the Congress of the Laity. The workshop, strangely enough, was on "Creativity in Religious Philanthropy," and was led by Robert W. Lynn, an executive with the Lilly Endowment, Inc., and a former seminary professor in the fields of history and education. Let me hasten to say I am not mounting a defense of religious philanthropy or an appeal to the laity to set up charitable foundations, although I believe in the former and would welcome the latter. I first want to summarize part of what Lynn said, then make an application that takes it out of the philanthropic arena.

Private foundations as we have them in our culture were, according to Lynn, outcroppings of the evangelical awakening of the nineteenth century. They, like many other voluntary associations, were set up for the amelioration of social ills, such as slavery or illiteracy. Many espoused and financed social causes—education for blacks or coal miners' daughters, literacy in Asia or nursery facilities for working mothers in Chicago. The early foundations, Lynn said, were mostly charities in the sense of distributing beneficence and, over the years, built up constituents—schools, agencies, and the like—dependent on them for operating subsidies.

Then in the early twentieth century, Lynn continued, came John D. Rockefeller, Jr., who was not interested in charity but in philanthropy. What is the difference? Charity, Lynn said, is bound to precedent, conditioned by dependencies established in the past. Philanthropy anticipates the future. Lynn recalled that in 1916 Rockefeller wrote an article in the *Saturday Evening Post* in which he announced he would give no more money to anything increasing denominational conflicts and divisions in American religion. He favored religious cooperation and set forth a vision of how he wanted to use the Rockefeller fortune to help bring the Kingdom of God on earth. Rockefeller's vision aside, philanthropy enjoys an independence from recipients that allows a foundation to be an early-warning system, to take social risks, Lynn explained.

Most—not all—major private foundations in America today are philanthropies, as distinct from charities, in Lynn's terms. (Any time a foundation says it no longer funds "business as usual" it is changing from a charity to a philanthropy.) Philanthropic foundations, Lynn said, are criticized from every side and the middle and are not without the problems that accompany the dispensation of grants. With all that, he went on, they have unequalled occasion for creativity, for exploring unpopular ideas or causes, and for engaging in work nobody else in society wants to do. They can monitor the on-coming problems and possibilities in society and focus attention and imagination. Foundations, Lynn added, can also live with an issue long enough to weigh the long-term effects or seek out alternative solutions because they can, if they will, resist the temptation to join the passing parade of fads and fashions. But the enterprise of philanthropy, Lynn warned, must acknowledge the possibility of failure, of dead ends, of picking the wrong issues.

Now what application does Lynn's description of philanthropy have for the laity as a moral force in society? The relevance of some of his remarks should be instantly evident. The Christian waits today for the breaking in of tomorrow; "this day" he looks for "that day": eschatological hope anticipates the future. Without big wealth, great power, or public prestige, individual lay Christians and groups of the laity can form a network to serve as a moral early-warning system. The moral horizon emerges out of the present. Surprises come along, but by and large we find out about ethical dilemmas in the on-coming future by knowing the pulse of people in our own communities as those communities collectively form a society. Let me suggest a rule of thumb for relating to the future: Tomorrow is to today as today is to yesterday, an almost simple-minded remark that carries a lot of truth. A war may break out on Thursday that we did not expect on Tuesday but in nine times out of nine and a half the ingredients for causing the war were there, and evident, on Monday. Tomorrow—and all that implies—contains the same reality that we hope in today, with the same unexpectedness that made today different from yesterday. Trends, as distinct from fads, usually marshal slowly. We need not rely solely on university research projects, polls, and pundits to enlighten us on the fears, expectations, and confusions—all of which affect the moral climate—of the American people. We ought to be enlightening the "authorities" of all kinds on the basis of our sensitivity to ourselves, our neighbors, and the wider community in which we live.

Because the Christ who is in us is also the Christ who is to come, we, the laity, can launch the unexpected. We can anticipate tomorrow today. We can investigate unpopular and popular causes. What are they really about? What has generated them? Is there validity to their grievances (and all causes have grievances)? We can think the causes through. What impact will they have on society if they are encouraged, or discouraged? We can do the work no one else wants to do, taking the church into the world—from developing rapport with juvenile offenders to asking the hard questions from the inside about impersonal business corporations.

Most of all, we can stick with the spiritual issues and moral problems that plague our society. Every one of us tires or bores easily. New energy, new excitement comes by finding a fresh interest. Race relations in America come up as an issue today and we are inclined to say, "But we took care of that in the nineteen sixties." Some work was done, yes, but all of us know the job is far from finished. It bothered me how some of the religious social activists of the sixties hopped, skipped, and jumped from civil rights to peace, to ecology, to farm workers, to prison reform, to the restructure of the university, always trying, it seemed, to stay at the front of the line. That mentality could not accomplish very much—it never stuck to anything long enough. It never took enough time to develop relationships. (And is the same mentality, I might add, that afflicts evangelism separated from church development and spiritual growth, though it comes from the opposite end of the political spectrum.) We can hardly be one-issue people given the plethora of moral crises. And yet we must accept our human limitations. We will find it necessary, no doubt, to distribute our energies, some of us working on morality in government, for example, some on justice in the marketplace, some on institutional renewal and others on the tone of the media, always keeping in touch, since all the moral issues of the day are interrelated. Keeping in touch on issues and something more: learning to trust each others' moral integrity as Christians even as we experience the theological and social tensions inherent in a pluralistic society.

The movement toward a more moral America will be uphill, as Mike Novak said in the conversation with James Reston. Climbing a real hill (even like some of those near Laity Lodge in our Texas' Hill Country) takes imagination—vision that it can be climbed; creativity—selection of a route; and hard work—achieving the vision. Will is the prerequisite. A will committed to God. I must, however, conclude here with a warning issued by Tom Howard, "The Christian vision has a paradoxical relation to history. To be Christian is to be obedient to Christ in the social sphere, but the Christian has this notion that the human enterprise will fall on its head. We could end up building Babylon instead of Jerusalem."

To put faith to work in the world, to connect personal and national morality is not to set our vision on a "heaven on earth" made by human hands. It is not even to "usher in" God's Kingdom. God alone is the usher of the eternal Kingdom, and *our* Jerusalems can become *our* Babylons.

Section C (in this chapter), following the Reston speech text, is a slightly abridged version of a talk given in a congress workshop by Justice Thomas M. Reavley, formerly of the Texas Supreme Court. It is placed here because it elaborates the theme of interconnection between personal and public morality. Reavley, as much as any person I know, is a living example of a lay Christian dedicated first to Christ and second to the common good. He has a rare perception of his own motivation and splendidly communicates his passion for Christian unity and for Christian initiatives to improve society.

Reavley was named to the Texas Supreme Court in nineteen hundred and sixty-eight after an outstanding career as an attorney. When in practice, he always made it part of his business to be engaged at all times in at least one no-fee project benefitting justice and the community. After a decade on the bench, he joined the faculty at the University of Texas Law School. Reavley is a member of the United Methodist Church.

B. PUBLIC MORALITY AND ENDURING PRINCIPLES

James Reston

I cannot speak for our friends from Canada and Mexico but I am convinced that in this country there is a longing for something precious that has been lost. We don't know quite what it is, but like our friend Zacchaeus, many of us are trying to see Jesus, but cannot see him for the darkness, or hear him for the noise.

Since this is a congress of the people, maybe we should begin with our own responsibility: the responsibility of the people. If we are living in a moral pigsty, as I believe, we cannot blame everything on the failure of the church, the schools, the politicians, the press, Jimmy Carter, or that handy catchall called "the system," though God knows there is blame enough to cover us all. Thomas Carlyle blamed the conditions that led to the French Revolution on every individual who had done less than his duty. Carlyle suggested that great calamities can befall a community, a nation, or a civilization, not only because of some blunder or idiocy in leadership, but also from the slow accumulation of petty betrayals or of small derelictions of personal duty.

It is popular these days to say that you cannot indict a whole people. But you cannot entirely acquit them, either, and it seems to me that this Congress of the Laity would be pointless if we did not begin with the belief that what we all do in our private lives and in our work has some bearing on the life of the Republic. One of the great ironies of the present age is that as the population of the Republic has grown, and its problems have become more numerous and complex, our people have slipped into the despondent belief that they have lost all influence. They have not. Recent history, I think, disproves this notion of impotence.

It was a constituency of the people who, protesting against the misery of the black man in the South, and against the Vietnam War, aroused the consciences of their brothers and sisters until they cried, "In the name of God, stop." The churches had been protesting for years, but it was the people who finally turned the government around and not vice versa.

PERSONAL AND NATIONAL MORALITY

It is hard for me to believe in a religious interpretation of history. I cannot, however, ignore the evidence that nations tend to get in trouble when they abandon their moral foundations. Nor can we ignore the fact that our most successful policies in this post-war era have been our generous peace treaties with Germany and Japan, and the Marshall Plan, which expressed pity and forgiveness inherent in the American spirit.

In short, I believe there is an unavoidable connection between personal and national morality. It cannot be an accident that this nation, which knew slavery was an abomination and a rebuke to all its religious and political principles, had to fight a savage war between the states to get rid of it. I know there are many explanations of our Civil War, commercial and political, but I cannot get away from the teachings in my parents' house that there was an element of judgment, of punishment, in this tragedy which cannot be explained wholly in economic or ethical terms.

Secular historians have explained the two world wars in terms of aggressive nationalism, economic competition, expanding navies, and the spirit of imperialism. I think the story is incomplete unless these wars are viewed also as civil war within what used to be called the old "Christian civilization." In the same way, school children learn that the Great Depression was brought on by the collapse of credit, by political isolation, and by economic protectionism. These are only modern words for human divisions and selfishness, which the religious prophets have warned us against for centuries.

STRUGGLE FOR THE IDEAL

It may be that my generation of journalists stumbled into their work at a special time in this nation's history. We should be cautious about reaching general conclusions from our own experience, but sometimes you must be personal to be understood.

For example, I keep holding to the remnant of my parents' belief, and for practical reasons. I simply feel guilty if I don't at least try. I am not hounded by nightmare visions of the Calvinist hell or interested in imposing my doubts and anxieties on others. It is simply that I would feel amputated and unfaithful if I did not reach out to what I know is a not wholly attainable ideal.

To many, this will sound like priggish moralizing, but in my experience, this endless struggle for the ideal, even if it fails, is worthwhile not only for an individual, but for a nation as well. There will always be a conflict between private morality and social morality. Personal religious or ethical values must inevitably clash with the purposes of the union, the corporation, the race, the community, state, or nation. This does not relieve the statesman of the obligation to try to bring about a reconciliation.

"When we speak as though there were a separate ethic for the statesman, a peculiar substance called policitical morality," Herbert Butterfield, the Cambridge religious historian once remarked, "we are already moving into a world of trick mirrors and optical illusions. . . . Certainly for my part, I do not see why in politics even the virtues I associate with the Christian religion should be suspended for a moment. . . ."

Obviously, many people would disagree. Prime Minister Begin of Israel and President Sadat of Egypt, both deeply religious men, would want to know how to reconcile their personal morality with their political responsibilities, and Butterfield would not hesitate to reply, as he said in lectures in this country:

> Here is a spacious and comprehensive human issue, at one of the epic stages in the world's history. It is a matter not to be settled in routine consultation between governments and their military experts who are always bent on going further and further in whatever direction they have already been moving.
>
> In such a crisis, even those of us who never had an superstituous belief in human rectitude will have some faith in humanity to assert—some heartthrob to communicate—so that, across all the iron curtains of the world, deep may call unto deep.
>
> There is aggression; there is tyranny; there is revolutionary ferment; but if we wish to civilize international affairs we must do more than arrogantly hold our own, merely meeting them

with their own weapons. Everything is going to depend in fact upon what we do over and above the work of self-defense. . . .[1]

Butterfield speculated, in that same context, "We wait, perhaps, for some Abraham Lincoln who will make the mightiest kind of liberating decision."

Some people put their faith in creeds, others in economic theories or temporal leaders, but I am talking about more mundane things. Aldous Huxley said:

> About the ideal goal of human effort, there exists in our civilization and, for nearly thirty centuries, there has existed a very general agreement. From Isaiah to Karl Marx, the prophets have spoken with one voice. In the Golden Age to which they look forward there will be liberty, peace, justice, and brotherly love. "Nations shall no more lift sword against nation"; "the free development of each will lead to the free development of all"; "the world shall be full of the knowledge of the Lord, as the waters cover the sea."
>
> With regard to the goal, there is and for a long time has been very general agreement. Not so with regard to the roads which lead to that goal. Here unanimity and certainty give place to utter confusion, to the clash of contradictory opinions, dogmatically held and acted upon with violence of fanaticism.[2]

Accordingly, I will stick to a few practical points from my own experience.

PROBLEM OF COMMUNICATION

I begin with the problem of communication. Everybody does these days. I'm sure that when Cain slew Abel, he blamed it on a failure of communication. As a reporter, I have come to know another, quite odd failure of communication.

There is, for example, a lot of kindness and even progress in this country that tends to be overlooked by the press.

---

[1] Herbert Butterfield, *International Conflict in the Twentieth Century: A Christian View* (London: Routledge and Kegan Paul Ltd. 1960), p. 90.

[2] Aldous Huxley, *Ends and Means* (New York: Harper and Brothers, 1937), p. 1.

Beyond this, there is a deeper paradox. The American press dramatizes the blunders and conflicts of the human race on the front pages, which the people read, and it denounces these blunders and conflicts on the editorial pages, which the people don't read. Then there is television. Television gives us heroes like Roger Staubach and Coach Tom Landry, but its chief contribution is to celebrate violence, to assail us with the pictures of what went wrong, news of contention and division, without trying too hard to condemn what it portrays with such immediate and vivid effect.

Some changes are occurring in world cummunications that do offer some hope. For example, the daily newspaper is adjusting to modern inventions and new forms of competition. I wish I could see the hand of the Lord in this and believe that newspaper publishers, like Saul on the road to Damascus, had been transformed by a blinding revelation. But that's not exactly what has happened.

In the first quarter of this century, the newspaper was the first purveyor of the news. Old geezers like me can remember the newsboys shouting "Extra!" in the night. No more. Science has changed all that. The radio took away from us our early-warning mission. Television took away the great descriptive story. How, even if we could write in iambic pentameter against the tyranny of the deadline, could we compete with television in describing the eulogies to Hubert Humphrey under the great dome of the capitol, when tens of millions could see the tears on Muriel Humphrey's cheeks?

So the press has had to find a different mission, or go broke. Since it couldn't compete with the radio in announcing events, or with the television, it had to deal with the *causes* and consequences of the daily turbulence in the world. In the process, the best of our newspapers have ventured, not far I admit, but some, into the analysis of human conduct, with ethical, philosophical, and even theological questions. This may be the best thing that has happened to the press in many years.

Newspapers have come to realize, as they should have long ago, that ideas are news; that wars begin in the minds of men and women; that the world is not changed primarily by politicians, who usually get more praise than they deserve and more blame than they can bear. But the world is being changed by the fertility of the human mind and body, by the birth of more human beings than we have the wisdom to feed, educate, and employ, and by physicians who are preserving life in infancy and prolonging it in old age.

This is the real news that should make us realize the common problems of the human family, and which has attracted a more thoughtful generation of reporters than any I have ever seen before. It has opened up "opposite editorial pages" to the creative, competent, moral leaders.

But one problem remains: Bad news still drives out good news, and somehow the people are entitled to hear about the best in America and not only the worst. Fortunately, we are now in the midst of the greatest printing revolution since the invention of movable type. With the comparatively inexpensive photocomposition computers and offset presses available in this modern world, it should be possible to give wider and wider circulation to the best minds and the best thought of the globe.

This isn't much in a time when reading is going out of style. Still, small steps can be taken. This congress could serve as a model for discussion at the local level. Our religious organizations are vast, potentially powerful networks for social, as well as religious, ideas. After all, this is how the women kept thought alive in the lonely communities of the American frontier.

PUBLIC INDIFFERENCE

Even if we were to perfect our communications system, our troubles would be far from over. Public indifference, pessimism, and even despair remain to be reckoned with—the failure of belief, perhaps even what Carlyle described as the dereliction of personal duty. The whole subject of the sacred and profane is so far beyond me that all I can hope to do is deal with the threshold questions. And, on that basis, it may help to remember that there has always been a strain of self-doubt and pessimism in the American character. For nearly a hundred years, the Republic was regarded as a dubious experiment, before people began to talk optimistically about the American Destiny, or the American Century.

"I tremble for my country when I reflect that God is just," Mr. Jefferson said in the seventeen eighties. John Adams wrote to Benjamin Rush in 1808: "Commerce, luxury, and avarice have destroyed every Republican government. We mortals cannot work miracles; we struggle in vain against the constitution and the course of nature."

Arthur Schlesinger, Jr., the historian, warned us during the Bicentennial not to think of our "innocence" or of ourselves as a chosen people. He said:

> No people who systematically enslaved black men and killed red men could be innocent. No people reared on Calvin and Tacitus, on Edwards and the *Federalist* could be innocent. No nation founded on invasion, conquest and slaughter could be innocent. No state founded by revolution and thereafter rent by civil war could be innocent. The Founding Fathers were not a band of saints. They were brave and imperturbable realists who committed themselves, in defiance of the available lessons of history and theology, to a monumental gamble.[3]

I don't mean to minimize the problems facing our own generation and particularly the young generation. I don't think I ever understood until my wife and I raised three boys what was meant in the Lord's Prayer by, "Lead us not into temptation." The temptations before the young today seem beyond the lusts of Sodom and Gomorrah. But each generation seems to complain about the wickedness of the age, and shudder at the fragility of human striving.

Even our most optimistic poet, Walt Whitman, wrote the following a little over one hundred years ago:

> Never was there more . . . hollowness at heart than at present, and here in the United States. Genuine belief seems to have left us. The underlying principles of the States are not honestly believed in. . . . The spectacle is appalling. We live in an atmo-

[3] Arthur Schlesinger, Jr., "America: Experiment or Destiny?", *American Historical Review,* Vol. 82, No. 3, June, 1977, p. 512.

sphere of hypocristy throughout. The men believe not in the women, nor the women in the men . . ., [and] the great cities reek with . . . robbery and scoundrelism.[4]

So much for the good old days. The main difference seems to be that the old boys wrote better.

There is always pessimism, but Whitman's despairing cry is not the picture of America I see today. I do see a crisis in the American family. The drug culture and the sexual revolution have not run their course. The good may be the end, but lies are often still the means, and there is certainly what Nicholas Berdyaev called a corrupting "inner, hidden falsity—falsity to oneself and to God which eludes detection and comes to be regarded as a virtue."

But I have a feeling that these gods have failed, too, and that the rising generation, observing the casualties of the sixties, has begun to wonder if not yet to reform.

That many are perplexed about the consequences of their own irreligion goes without saying. Having lost their faith, they have lost certainty that their lives are significant. Having inherited the kingdoms of this world they sought, they are dissatisfied with the world they inherited and are haunted by the need to believe in something. Walter Lippman noted this long ago in *A Preface to Morals:* "What most distinguishes them [the young], is not their rebellion against the religion and moral code of their parents, but their disillusionment with their own rebellion. It is common for young men and women to rebel, but that they should rebel sadly and without faith in their own rebellion, that they should distrust the new freedom no less than the old certainties— that is something of a novelty."[5]

Still, I believe in the theory of the remnant; that is, in a growing minority that clings to enduring principles, if only in self-defense. We may not be a very religious, but we are a

---

[4] Walt Whitman, "Democratic Vistas" (1871). Reprinted in *Complete Poetry and Selected Prose,* James F. Miller, Jr., ed. (Boston: Houghton Mifflin, 1959), p. 461.

[5] Walter Lippman, *A Preface to Morals* (New York: The Macmillan Co., 1929), p. 17.

very practical people. If things don't work we tend to abandon them quicker than most. And one of the enviable qualities of the American people is that they have no memory. There is, for example, very little anti-Japanese or anti-German feeling here a generation after the last war.

Therefore, let me end by quoting someone who can put all this in a better perspective than I: Reinhold Niebuhr in *The Irony of American History:*

> There are no simple congruities in life or history. The cult of happiness erroneously assumed them. . . . But all such strategies cannot finally overcome the fragmentary character of human existence. The final wisdom of life requires not the annulment of incongruity but the achievement of serenity within and above it.
>
> Nothing that is worth doing can be achieved in our lifetime; therefore we must be saved by hope. Nothing which is true or beautiful or good makes complete sense in any immediate context of history; therefore we must be saved by faith. Nothing we do, however virtuous, can be accomplished alone; therefore we are saved by love. No virtuous act is quite as virtuous from the standpoint of our friend or foe as it is from our standpoint. Therefore we must be saved by the final form of love which is forgiveness.[6]

C. WHAT TO DO ABOUT THE WORLD'S FAULTS?

Thomas M. Reavley

Why do anything about the world's faults except laugh at them? Why do anything except educate ourselves thoroughly so we can step aside . . . and prove how much smarter we are than politicians and people who try to run

[6] Reinhold Niebuhr, *The Irony of American History* (New York: Charles Scribner's Sons, 1962), pp. 62–63.

hospitals and schools and who try to improve the community? Why not just establish how much wiser we are by pronouncing the immiment doom, then advertise to all that we'll wait and in our faith there will be a better day in heaven?

Personally, I would have no interest in reform, in making anything any better, if I had no faith about the sources, about the eternal design—if I did not feel I am called. That is not to say enormous contributions have not been made by men and women who lacked faith, who lacked the Christian faith in particular. . . . There are brave, sooner or later bitter souls, I expect, who make contributions toward correcting the world's faults despite lack of faith in an overarching design. Not me. I could not. . . . If I am simply an accidential collocation of atoms, a descendant of something that somehow happened to climb out of the ooze, why exert myself? Why save the scenery just in case there is somebody else who accidentially comes along in the next generation?

Andrei Sokolov in Harrison Salisbury's *Gates of Hell,* which I understand is true to the life of Aleksandr Solzhenitsyn, is back from labor camp discussing his experience with his old Marxist friend. He tells him about a Father Ivan, who endured horrors but whose example meant so much to the other prisoners because of his faith. The Marxist friend is surprised that his comrade has acquired the Christian faith. Sokolov says, "No man can really face his fatherland without true faith."

I cannot face my country, my community, most of my neighbors, at least a lot of them, or the faults of the world without a faith in creation and the Creator who gives enough enduring significance to it all to justify our efforts in the common causes to make improvements—to save our cities and our communities and our society.

Direction? Goal . . . ? I have one from the Scripture. The same message is in several places in the writings of Paul, but I usually quote from Ephesians, the first chapter, which, as I understand it, was written not just to the Ephesians but to all Christian churches of all ages. . . . It is the divine plan that in the fulness of time all things in earth and in heaven will be united in Christ, under God as we know Him in

Christ (Eph. 1:10). Then, that marvelous fourth chapter, about the different gifts. The parts of the one body are not all alike. We're not talking about sameness. . . . We all have our different talents and assignments, gifts, but we seek the unity of faith and the knowledge of the Son of God. We seek maturity, no longer children being tossed to and fro by every wind of doctrine, every come-today-and-gone-tomorrow fad and fashion, but growing up into Him who is the head, the Christ, in whom the body is knit together . . . and built up in love.

You know, as much as Ephesians means to me, and as many times as I've tried to think about it, and speak to it, only recently have I realized this unity is not something that you and I build; called by God, serving God, with God, here on earth, bridging the chasms, trying to create peace and order. I realized, of course, that the unity already exists; not throughout our lives, not throughout my town or yours, but the unity is here: "In Him all things hold together." (Col. 1:17)

So it seems to me, I must, I can do no other, but open myself, allow myself to be part of that unity; to let the spirit of God Almighty, that Holy Spirit, unite me, and me with it, as predicate to my efforts to fix some toggle switch, to speed up the criminal or civil justice system, to simplify and make just these human systems, moving always toward unity, starting in my hometown.

I give due credit to enlightened intellectuals, people like Walter Lippman who, perhaps to his satisfaction, wrote in *A Preface to Morals* why and how we put together a code of ethics without God. These are brave servants of society who can do that. I cannot. It just won't work; it won't wash. I have to have faith or I don't care about the world's faults, except to make fun of them or to find some witty way to predict the doom of it all.

CYNICISM ABOUT INSTITUTIONS

I want to talk about what seems to me as great an obstacle as we have to improving the world, or our society, at least. I expect this obstacle is timeless and not limited to any one society, but it certainly afflicts us, with post-Vietnam and post-Watergate complicating the problem. When you speak to young people and you hear them . . . express their cynicism about the institutions of government, about all politicians, what do you say? . . .

People say to me: "You're in public office. . . . How can you be a Christian?" As if the twain could never meet. What do you say?

Let me mention a couple of things I have said.

I say, sometimes, you must work at your perspective on those people in the institutions, in politics, as well as your perspective on yourself. Why are you so sure that the president and the generals and members of Congress are always venial and self serving? Do you think you know enough about all the people in public life to make that assumption? (It's like the fellow who saw an Indian following another Indian through the forest and concluded that all Indians always walk in single file.) Do you know enough politicians to decide all are venial?

In my experience, there are all kinds of people in every endeavor. Take Joe, a student at such and such a school. . . . You know that some teachers are good and some not quite so good. I think most of them try, but occasionally you may find one who does not. Would you categorize all teachers, in one fell swoop, as being there only to hold down a job, to work for retirement pay? I have never been in any kind of corporate endeavor of any size where there were not some people trying to improve the services; in the church, in the schools, in the legislature, in the Texas judiciary, some people are trying to put forth that extra effort to make improvements. . . . And usually you also have people interested only in themselves, their power, their pension, their financial gain, higher office, all the words they can get in the press. And there are the in-between people who have learned how to do what must be done and are willing to do that and only that and are hesitant, at best, about any change that threatens their status or standing.

What you do, if you dispose of all politicians, is not only a cop-out, stopping before you know enough about the legislators, for example, to pronounce any judgment, but it is worse than that. That sort of cynicism, that sort of declaration of hopelessness about politicians, delivers the legislature into the hands of the demogogues and self-seekers. To improve anything in any community takes thrust because there is this inertia. . . . And the only way to get thrust is through some sort of popular support. If you have no discrimination at all—all politicians in the same pot—you deprive the people who are trying to do something better of the support they need, and of the necessary thrust.

Anyone who has been in any real fights, whether in the city council or a legislature has had occasions when just the people who ought to be giving the support quit you because for some reason they thought they were righteous and you were tainted. And there you were locked in embrace with the kind of confrontation one goes through to cope with the problems of this world.

QUICK CONDEMNATIONS

I sometimes say, about perspective on ourselves, why are we so quick to condemn? Why do we talk about *all* politicians being crooked, and *all* teachers this and preachers that and the lawyers so and so? Why won't we try to discriminate and see there are all kinds in all professions? It is because of this damnable idea that somehow we exalt ourselves by putting someone else down. It's more than competition. It's the feeling of being put upon because the laborers in the vineyard who worked a few hours less got the same pay, as if we were abused by the grace and generosity of the landlord, the Lord of life.

Why do we have to compare ourselves with other people constantly? Why can't we see our community in kinship? If community is important, and it's God's will we're trying to serve, who gets the credit and who is smarter is not all that important. If determining who gets the credit is not important to you, you sure can do a lot more to help the faults of this world. I don't believe anything stalls progress to correct the faults of our institutions and our society nearly so much as the fussing and fighting over who's going to get the credit.

There they were on the road to Jerusalem, and the first thing the disciples start fighting over is the pecking order. At the Last Supper, just before our Lord goes to trial, God Almighty on trial; just before the resurrection, the event that will separate B.C. from A.D., the disciples who must carry on mission to save the world and meet its faults—they're arguing over who's going to have priority in the next kingdom. But that's not the Christian way. . . .

We need a perspective on our own purpose in condemning others, and, let me say, when we judge, we judge ourselves, for by that judgment we judge, we are judged. . . . I'm no Pollyanna, but when we point fingers at everybody in politics, such condemnations show the hopelessness, the lack of direction the speaker holds in his own heart.

Chapter Nine

A WORLD OF
ORGANIZATIONS

A. VENTURES IN THE IMPERFECT

Judge Reavley is right. Cynicism toward political and social institutions is rampant, and, it seems to me, a part of the reason is summed up in the opening paragraph of Peter Drucker's congress address: Organizations established in perpetuity dominate virtually every area of life. Many of us, younger and older, male and female, are nostalgic for days when heroic individualism counted. Among the most touted media celebrities are independent entertainment entrepreneurs, "free agent" athletes, maverick politicians and nonestablishment authors—people who go out and make it on their own (never mind that such persons are usually quite as dependent on the existence of the organizations as their less venturesome neighbors). However, I detect a more substantial reason for the cynicism. We are disillusioned with a network of institutions and organizations that have promised more than can be delivered; namely, a near-perfect society.

At least until recently and perhaps still, Americans suffered from the disease of easy optimism. We, as a people, want to "win" and believe we can win in absolutely everything, including the construction of a problem-free society. Such optimism has resulted in our neglect of, or our superficial agreement to, the theological doctrines of "the fall" and original sin. Original sin—and I mean here simply that sin of which we are culpable as part of "fallen" creation—is treated by most Amerians as an ailment afflicting everyone but us, as though we are somehow miraculously cured by New World balm. Some streams of our theological heritage have done great disservice by deemphasizing sin, evil, and the fall. In this here-and-now, this "until . . . ," even optimistic Americans operate in large part in darkness and shadows as we organize society and try to make it work. Our social vision is not 20-20. None of our institutions are perfect. How could they be? Few, if any, of their architects and custodians are perfect. I have never known or heard of a single person whose wings began to sprout in this life (although I have known some few who claimed halos), and no institution we have was let down by golden ropes from heaven.

Yet I totally agree with Reavley's distaste for cynicism toward institutions, such as government, education, the law, business, and medicine. Anarchy works only for angels, John Van de Water said in a congress workshop, but recalling Revelation 12:7–12 (the passage on the revolt in heaven) anarchy does not work for angels either. Ours is a society of organizations, as Drucker says. What we have built in America is an interconnecting system of public and private institutions, which discharge virtually every task in the community. For better or worse (and I think for the better in our day and age), that is what we have, and the diversification and decentralization within the system seems to me to be its greatest strength. The problem, as I see it, is the repetitive impersonality of institutions created, as Drucker says, for "perpetuity." That is one factor in why I could never abandon a religious interpretation of history and society, specifically a religious interpretation linking transcendence and immanence. I believe the power to transform all systems comes from outside them, from the personal, just as the power to transform the world is based outside, in God. At the same time, transcendent power operates immanently, inside the system, just as God is in the world through Christ. In faithfulness to Christ, the challenge to the laity is to be "in" but not "of" institutions and systems, to be morally creative within our own organizations and as we relate to others. We have only begun to explore the Christian potential for changing, for personalizing, institutional life. When

Jesus spoke of structures, of "discipling the nations," he meant far more than we have understood. The prospects ahead on this front are exciting but often appear overwhelming; we resist despair best in concentrating on the organizations of our own particular leadership responsibility.

Drucker (Section B of this chapter) primarily describes the roles of the organization in modern society. Various Congress of the Laity workshops explored the moral problems lay Christians encounter in relating to specific forms of social organizton. Let me cite examples of corporate responsibility, labor-management relations and taxation, lifting from workshop presentations points the laity must ponder from the perspectives of faith and morality.

"Can an enterprising democratic system such as ours survive in a no-growth mode?" asked Charles Robinson, former deptuy secretary of state, in a session on "International Corporate Social and Ethical Responsibility." Robinson, now an investment banker, said the United States faces in the next decade a growth rate of only 2 to 3 percent or less, while it has been fluctuating at around 5 percent. The American economic community, according to Robinson, has failed to realize the acceleration of change and the growth of economic problems over the past thirty years, so that today sharper vision, more courage and economic belt-tightening are necessary on the home front. What does this mean for the fulfillment of the national moral obligation to developing nations of Africa, Asia, and Latin America? he asked.

Robinson saw no chance of the United States ever elevating the world's entire population to our level of affluence. Instead of efforts along those lines, he advocated a total change in global relationships. To prepare for that change, he listed three "crucial truths" that corporations must acknowledge: (1) a new wave of "interdependence" around the globe; (2) the proliferation of independent nations which cannot stand alone economically; and (3) the growing involvement in the world economy of states which do not respond to free-market forces but rather to political motives. It is critical, said Robinson, for business leaders to realize the interdependence of nations and peoples, to contribute to the resolution of international problems and to employ a strong sense of ethics in all undertakings. "If we can exhibit these qualities, then this global society of ours will contribute to the pool of human creativity so vital to us all," he added. Robinson was also distressed that United Sates companies would resort to bribery in their international dealings, and recommended business-government cooperation in drafting a code of conduct for multinational corporations. "In an interdependent world," he said, "it becomes unrealistic to try to get government out of business's hair. Instead, business and government will learn to work together for the mutual benefit of both."

John Van de Water, a mangement consultant, raised similar moral issues in a workshop on "Creative Approaches to Labor-Management Relations." How, he asked, do we overcome the unfortunate fact that in labor-management disputes both sides spread false rumors designed to serve self-interests? How do managers work creatively with employees to help individuals realize and accomplish their potentials? How do we overcome the mentality of "labor versus management" and cultivate the idea that both are interdependent?

As a consultant to management, Van de Water spoke with unswerving directness to that group, "Management must be honest; we need, not relative honesty, but absolute honesty." He said he feels labor unions, which represent about 24 percent of the national work force, have too much power, but despite that he saw no reason for management to withhold pertinent information from employees. Unionization, he commented, is the business of neither management nor the union; it is the business of the employees. And all too often, when strikes and worse occur, management fails to ask where it went wrong, he said. "We must not foment a situation of militant materialism," Van de Water told his workshop. "Self-righteousness will build a barrier to the dialogue we need."

Van de Water would banish from labor-management relations the instincts to blame others and to punish or destroy. He would strive toward solutions fair and just for all concerned. Speaking as a Christian to fellow Christians in business, he said, "To live like Christians in this world, we must put our spiritual principles first, our moral and ethical principles second, our human and social values third, and our material values last."

What about morality in relation to something as complex as taxation? Vester T. Hughes, Jr., a noted tax attorney, led a congress workshop on "The Morality of Taxation." The congress coincided with early rumblings of what has come to be called the "tax revolt of 1978" (most dramatic in the California referendum lowering property taxes). Hughes said that how people feel about government expenditures determines in some measue how they feel about taxation. He was not sure such feelings provide a meaningful basis for tax decisions, not in isolation anyway.

The lawyer's judgment was that the United States tax system incorporates principles a moral system should contain, features such as like taxation of like cases, tax authorization by the citizens, higher rates for luxury items, public announcement of what is taxed, and progressivity in taxing income. But he enumerated many unanswered tax-related questions with moral dimensions. What is fair, and who determines the defintion? Should taxation be used to encourage economic growth? At what point are poverty or education ignored for the sake of long-range growth? What about the morality of tax administration, even if the system is sound?

I could go on and on listing questions that illustrate moral problems in the world of organizations and social institutions. Those I have picked from the congress workshops are mind boggling, yet they must not be ignored. We, the Christian laity, cannot sit back and leave all these matters to government and politicians, to corporations and to the universities. We are too large a part of the people who run the government, the corporations, and the educational systems. Like it or not, the questions are squarely on our shoulders.

B.   THE ROLE OF
THE ORGANIZATION

Peter Drucker

Within this century, our society has become a society of organizations. Most every major task in the community is being discharged in and through a large organization established for perpetuity—school, hospital, government agency, research laboratory, labor union, organizations on service, business, and a good many more. If you go back seventy-five years, they were, at best, embryonic. Within this very short period in human history, these organizations have become the major opportunities for human beings, especially the educated ones. About nineteen out of every twenty men and women with an education beyond high school become part of an organization and remain there all their working lives. There they find not only a living but also the opportunity for contribution to society.

These are very great changes, and after having observed organizations for a very long time, I am reasonably sure that we do not understand them. What we think we know about management is largely folklore and superstition. I only hope that fifty years hence our grandchildren, when they look at the way we have been running our institutions, will see how stupid their ancestors were. We are much like the physicians of the eighteenth century who, when the patient didn't get better, blamed the patient.

RESULTS ON THE OUTSIDE

When you look at these organizations of ours, their results are only on the outside. On the inside, every one of them are only efforts, attempts, good intentions, costs, wastes, irritations, and bad tempers. But it doesn't matter whether the nurses in the hospital like the hospital or not. What matters is whether the patient gets out alive. What matters is not whether the faculty is harmonious. What matters is whether the kids learn once in a great while. And what matters in the business is really not the internal harmony.

There is a wonderful letter of St. Augustine's that I always quoted in my earlier unregenerate days when I taught philosophy and religion. We don't know to whom he wrote it, but obviously to a lady in the community who berated him because he bought his sandals from the pagan shoemaker in town rather than the perfectly god-fearing shoemaker. St. Augustine, who was Bishop of Hippo in North Africa, wrote back, "You know, my dear, in my job I have to walk a great deal, all over, up and down the desert, and I can't afford to wear sandals that give me blisters." There is no correlation between "saintliness" and "knowing how to make sandals."

That's a very profound insight. What matters is that the sandals fit and that the fellow who makes them knows how to make sandals. If he doesn't know how to make them, don't patronize him because of the goodness of his heart.

What matters in any organization is the impact it makes on the outside, because it exists only for the sake of the contribution. So in all management, whether you are talking of a government agency or of the shoe company, or of anything in between, you are concerned with the contribution made to the outside, the service it renders—whether it's in terms of customers or patients or citizens. You always have to watch lest the inside become an end in itself, lest the inside makes you forget why you are around, why you are being paid, why you do the work.

The thing to watch for in an organization is not slipshodness, not even arrogance; the thing to watch for is people becoming so enamored of the work they do that they forget why they do it, like a very old friend of mine, a very good doctor, who if he hasn't removed a gall bladder for a week begins to be very unhappy and looks for gall bladders to take out. Now, that's the big thing to watch out for with institutions that focus on their work. The work becomes the end purpose, and one forgets that the work is done for the sake of the result. Yet one has to maintain skill, craftsmanship, or lose it fast.

There is, of course, an internal dimension because when we say "organization," it's a short sentence, we mean people. When you look at white mice in a laboratory, you don't call them an organization. Organizations are people, human beings who are never, in modern organizations, "members." I am very careful not to use that word. I hear it all the time—"members of our company." It's the wrong term. Members by definition do not exist away from their body. You cut off a hand and it isn't a hand. People exist primarily "outside" in modern organization. They exist as parents and Christians and Americans and members of the school board and fathers of Little Leaguers and what have you—ninty-nine other exposures, each of them meaningful and real. It is only through one dimension, and a very important one, but only one, that persons are also *in* the organization.

THE WORK BOND

Yet the organization does have more impact in many ways on people than almost any other human bond, especially as people get older. As we advance in years, the work bond becomes not the most important community bond, but its importance increases. While the other bonds remain significant, they don't provide the daily stimulus of the work bond. Of all the bonds of life, it is the most lasting and most flexible, simply because it fits best with what we can do.

Here is Jim. I have been working with Jim for eighteen years, and I never see him except "on the job." I never exchange more words than are necessary with him, and I really am not very fond of Jim, but I respect him and we get along fine on the job. When he dies or retires, I'll miss him terribly. And here is Joe. Joe is my closest friend and his wife and my wife are inseparable and our children grew up together, and we take our vacations together. Work orders our lives, too. My relationships with Jim and Joe are both easily within the work bond, which of all human bonds has the greatest plasticity, is the easiest to control.

The work bond has a great deal of flexibility and a great deal of control by the individual. It becomes more and more important as we get older. While it is only one exposure, it's the one where, increasingly, the decision is being made as to whether an individual really contributes, really can discharge what he can do, or whether he is likely to be wasted and misallocated. The parable of the talents is, I think, the most unambiguous of all the biblical parables. (Each steward is entrusted according to his own ability.) Today, it is very largely up to the organization to think through, to discover what a person can really do. What are his or her strengths? What performance can one achieve, and where does each belong so he or she can perform?

GOOD FOR WHAT?

People in organizations, whether it's a university or a hospital or a business, spend a great deal of time in personnel selection.

Actually, there is no point in "selecting" personnel right out of school. You know absolutely nothing about the people, except the schoolmaster's grades. No schoolmaster has ever paid much attention to little Suzy, except whether she learns her French irregular verbs, and there is no correlation between speaking French and knowing irregular verbs. Little Suzy gets a B+ in irregular verbs because that's all she had to learn that year . . . and it's all you know when she applies for a job. At that stage, the young people know nothing about the organization and the world of work. What you can tell them makes no sense; they lack the experience for it to be meaningful.

I think that if we selected personnel at random we'd be just as well off and, sometimes, better off than in the way we try to do it now. I once taught statistics in my ill-spent life, which I have spent largely learning nothing and teaching everything. A very old law of statistics says that if a method doesn't have a much better chance to come out than random, take random—it's cheaper. So selection could just as well be made "at random." Then, instead of forgetting about the persons, the job of placement and development begins. The job of personnel officers is to find out what a person can do, what his or her strengths are. And don't ever say he or she is a "good" man or a "good" woman. Christians are not allowed to say that, it's the recording angel's job.

"Good for what?" is always the question. Accept the fact that the Lord has fashioned us for his purposes. This always includes being good for something, and *not* good for many more things. Everybody is capable of doing one thing very well and very few of us are capable of doing more than that.

Just imagine if Mozart had been asked to manage a hotel. Just imagine! Good for what? This is the challenge, the opportunity, in organizations. Organizations exist to make strengths productive and weaknesses irrelevant.

The great challenges to organizations, challenges I don't think we have addressed yet, are the same as their purpose: to make human strength, to make individual strength, to make personal strength effective and weakness irrelevant by looking for what a person can perform, can do. What does he or she need to learn to get the most out of this strength, to do it on the job where one can perform through his strengths and where his weaknesses won't matter?

That Mozart couldn't run a hotel didn't really matter when he sat down at the piano. So, let me conclude with a personal story. I started out to be a professional musician— and I once said to my very good music teacher, "How come that almost every composer's music is being transcribed except Mozart's? Here are transcriptions of Bach for the big Philadelphia Symphony Orchestra and . . . transcriptions of operas, but there are no Mozart transcriptions."

My teacher laughed and said, "Well, why don't you try it?" He gave me a string trio—violin, viola, and cello. It looked very simple. "Pick any instruments you want to transcribe it for—piano, orchestra, anything," he said. I came back two weeks later. "How is it going?" he asked. I said, "It's very easy, but it never sounds right."

He laughed some more. "That's exactly what everybody has found. It is very unique that every part of Mozart is perfect for the instrument he chose. He put the strength of the instrument to work, and the limitations disappear, become irrelevant. If it is for viola you can't transcribe it because it is right for the viola. It is perfect, and the sound it has on the viola can't be found in anything else. No one has ever been able to transcribe Mozart."

This is using organization to make people perform. This is looking at each of us as a special instrument fashioned by the Lord for his purposes, finding the purpose and making each of us effective in contribution and service. This is the challenge, the promise, the excitement ahead of us in making our organizations perform—perform as instruments of creation, of creativity, of service, and of excellence.

C.   DARKNESS AND THE LIGHT

Much of what Drucker said about the nature and role of organizations in modern life could be applied to the church and to other religious institutions. However, since most of the laity are not employed under religion's auspices, his address was properly kept to the secular sphere. The conversation after the talk was especially relevant to lay Christians struggling with ethical questions in relation to their own organizations.

Peter Berger was somewhat bothered by Drucker's stress on the outside results of organizations. He wondered whether a prior question is not that of an organization's purpose. Organizations, he noted, can have "absolutely odious purposes." Berger was further concerned about a contradiction he heard in Drucker and felt in himself. He agreed that we live in a world of organizations that no one, including the experts, understands. He agreed that in this era of organizations each person should do what he or she can, and do it faithfully. But, he asked, if we do not understand the world, how can people know what they are good for? How do we know a "good" performance? We most often operate, Berger said, out of "the ethics of ignorance."

Tom Howard wondered if what Drucker was saying about discovering and maximizing the strength of people as they work together does not fly in the face of the contemporary emphasis on individual self-discovery. To find one's personal "identity" and move on from there is what about 90 percent of modern people seem to expect, he said.

Drucker responded, first to Berger, then Howard:

> I have never said, "Anything that works is right." I think the purpose lies outside of the institution, and one can and should very clearly distinguish between what is constructive and what is destructive and what is merely factual in the largest category. . . .
>
> I do a great deal of work with health care and, believe me, the questions of health care are neither economic nor managerial, but fundamentally ethical. Our health-care problems are not the costs . . . or the operation of that most complicated institution man has ever tried to design—the modern hospital. *The* problem is who makes the decision when prolonging life and preventing death are no longer the same thing—when the two become further and further apart. We can postpone death, in many cases, but can't prolong life in any sense of the word. The absence of life has always been considered death and the absence of death [considered] life. This is no longer correct. There are ethical decisions to be made, and I am only very grateful that the good Lord has spared me making them. I would not want to make them, but they must be made. There you have the issue—a value question which is not pragmatic and which one has to think through in terms of first principles. . . . I don't think it's given to human beings to do good; it is only given to us to try not to do evil. I come from three or four hundred years of very stern Calvinists, and when one tries to focus oneself on using the strength one has in performance and in service, it's the only thing one has.

As for this talk about "finding" oneself, I think one finds oneself through the echo. We are created in somebody else's image and so one has to see the echo. Images cannot be seen any other way, and I think very seriously there is grave danger in this emphasis on finding oneself without discipline. For most of us, the only discipline we can really use is the discipline that is at least partially outside. If you go to the Jesuit Fathers, who know a good deal about spiritual discipline, they are not going to allow you into a novitiate without the novice master.

Gary Demarest brought into the conversation the question of the transcendental dimension in the use of gifts and talents in the world. He pointed out that evangelical Protestants have usually held that the experience of God "within us" is a factor in success, at least in the elevation of potential. He put the question specifically to Peter Berger, who has written about the transcendent dimensions of life, notably in a book called *A Rumor of Angels*.

BERGER: I think the fact that I am not an evangelical, the fact that my background is Lutheran, is quite relevant, because I doubt very much whether the transcendental dimension of the Christian life is going to give us an awful lot of direct guidance for the kind of problem (organizational life) we are addressing. . . . I am not sure there is a clear, Christian way of explaining why capitalism is a superior system to socialism, which I happen to believe, but not for Christian reasons. . . . Well, I think the transcendental dimension comes in and, if I may, I'll take the liberty of coming back to the phrase I used earlier, "the ethics of ignorance." In our social involvements, whether it's the new organizations . . . or in types of situations that may be older and more understandable, we really don't know what we are doing, we don't understand the complex in which we find ourselves. We never know the consequences of our actions. I think what the Christian faith—the transcendental dimension of life—can do is to allow us to stumble around in the dark and yet not become ignorant. And that is terribly important.

. . . .

MICHAEL NOVAK: . . . In this "ethics of ignorance," we need, especially in the Christian community, to emphasize that the causes in which we believe most, particularly those in the political, social, economic order, might in the long run of history turn out to be the wrong causes. . . . It's part of the transcendental vision to remember that whichever side you're on, you could be wrong. . . . You need to have a faith in reconciliation and in redemption because your own efforts could so easily be mistaken. . . .

DRUCKER: Mike, you are raising the question of which is worse, the arrogance of the theologians who believe in God or the arrogance of theologians who don't? I long ago decided that I prefer the theologians who believe in God, because they might be saved, and our present intellectual elite theologians who do not believe in God cannot be saved. They are damned. That we have known for a very long time. And if you have to have the arrogance of theologians . . . you'd better believe in Higher Authority!

NOVAK: In terms of belief in God and what it entails in economics and the rest of the world, we do live in a darkness, and the darkness of the believer is very much like that of the unbeliever. . . .

. . . .

DEMAREST: Isn't there a biblical theme, however, of light dispelling darkness . . .

BERGER: . . . This light . . . is, I think, a promise of redemption, which is not easily available in this world as it is now. . . . I think that one thing that differentiates evangelicals from other Christians is that you people are a bit more sure of this light . . . and we—a lot of other traditions— are less certain, more nervous about it.

Time had run out. Berger hoped the group could return to the issue of darkness and the light but it did not come up again, not in those terms anyway. I will not presume here to conclude with a neat theological consensus, for that would be quite false. Some Christians ardently believe the light of God, of Christ, is in the world or in them pushing back the darkness. Others are more nervous and, as Berger said, see redemption more as a promise or, as Novak said at one point, come to believe in a higher power of light through the experience of darkness. Christians, I am sure, will go on for aeons debating darkness and light in terms of Scripture, experience, reason, tradition, and anything else that offers means of communication.

As this whole matter concerns the lay pilgrimage and vocation in the world of organizations, I would say only this: I believe those who are convinced they have the light and those expecting promised light can walk together on the same road.

Chapter Ten

FAMILY AFFAIRS

A. HOPE FOR THE HOME?

No institution is more vital to society than the home and none a greater challenge to Christian creativity. Hope and despair intersect daily in our families. Some voices today claim the family is falling apart. Others say it is in fairly good shape. I cannot mediate the distance between those positions. I would say the family is a durable, an essential institution currently at an "edge of despair"—in transition. What the outcome of the transition will be, I know not, but it seems to me that the home—the family—is an arena of Christian witness and loving service too often forgotten when we speak of Christian social responsibility.

The "corporate honcho" in chapter seven, page 117, was looking for help in relating his faith to his home, to his teenage son, who never sees him. That lay Christian is not alone. We read a great deal about what is wrong with the family but much less about what people are doing to creatively cope with the tensions and crises. I expect that is because it is always easier to describe a sociological situation than to improve it.

For the Christian laity, social responsibility is not solely "out there" in the world of work and civic affairs. It is also found "close in" at hearth and board. There are far too many situations similar to that depicted in one segment of the "Six American Families" series shown on public television in 1977. An active church member, a committed layman, spends so much time in community work on behalf of the handicapped that he totally neglects and, to a degree, alienates his family. The same tragedy can arise when "church work," the religious organization itself, produces husband-wife and parent-child estrangement.

The family is under intense study today. One new area of inquiry is the impact on domestic life of the women's movement, with its increase of working mothers. Cynthia Wedel, director of volunteers for the American Red Cross and a president of the World Council of Churches, led a Congress of the Laity workshop on that issue. A topic social scientists have had longer to ponder and investigate is that of the absent or emotionally unavailable father. For years, at least since World War II, upward mobile, professionally engaged fathers have been increasingly shadowy figures in their homes and to their children. Many are simply never home.

It may take several years to determine the impact on family and children of two working parents, since the increase of working mothers is fairly recent. Alert researchers already know, rather conclusively, the ramifications of one absent or unavailable parent—the father. Simply put, the question of who's raising the children and how is of critical importance to the whole of society and is a problem the Christian laity had best not ignore. If the home as we have known it is bankrupt, we would do well to acknowledge the fact and try to come up with some suitable alternatives for intimate interpersonal relationship and child raising; but, if we feel any loyalty to the historic one man–one woman arrangement and feel any responsibility—any love—for offsprings, we may need to alter society to save the home.

A most informative paper on "The Professional Man and His Family: Areas of Conflict" was presented in a congress workshop by Armand M. Nicholi, M.D., a psychiatrist and member of the faculty at the Harvard Medical School. Nicholi is a foremost national authority on the psychological effect on children of the missing or inaccessible father. He is also a physician convinced that the Scriptures have more to offer modern psychiatry than anyone has dared dream. A part of his presentation follows. For space reasons, a lengthy single case history has been omitted.

B. THE PROFESSIONAL MAN AND HIS FAMILY: AREAS OF CONFLICT

Armand M. Nicholi, M.D.

Regardless of differences in our cultural, social, educational, or religious backgrounds, we all share the experience of being a child and, for good or evil, spending our days of childhood in the context of the family. Here the seed is sown for what we become as adults. Once adults, most of us marry and begin life in a second family. As we grow older, we find ourselves, as grandparents, part of still another family. So for most of us, most of our lives are lived within the framework of the family. And within this framework, our inner conflicts have their roots.

I would like to share a few impressions from my clinical experience and a few findings from my research and the research of others pertaining to the family. . . . Let me begin with some general observations from my clinical work that have relevance. First, during the past ten years I have noticed a marked change in the type of problems that bring young people to a psychiatrist. Previously, a great many came because of excessive inhibition of impulses. That is still common but not the major complaint. Today, the opposite holds true. A majority come because of inability to control impulses, which leads to many consequences. And people in my field attribute this lack of control to the declining influence of the father in the American home. Secondly, I have noticed what appears to be an increased incidence of problems in sexual identity among young people. This has particular relevance in that recent research shows a statistically significant higher incidence of cold, distant, rejecting, and inaccessible fathers within the family background of these individuals.

WHAT RESEARCH SHOWS

A. A research interest of mine during the past few years has been the large number of young people who drop out of college and out of society as well. About half of the seven and one-half million United States college students will drop out, about one million of them for psychiatric reasons. My sample consisted of one thousand five hundred young men who dropped out of Harvard over a five-year period. Two characteristics of the group leaving for emotional reasons that relate to our discussion are: (1) a marked isolation from their parents, especially their fathers, and (2) an overwhelming, paralyzing apathy. Many experienced an utter and complete lack of motivation.

In addition, among those who dropped out for psychiatric reasons and suffered the most serious illnesses, i.e., those hospitalized and diagnosed schizophrenic, a large number lost one or both parents through death. When compared with control groups, this finding proved highly significant statistically. This provided our first clue that there might be some relationship between a missing parent and emotional illness.

B. In another project, I interviewed a large number of young people who took hallucinogenic drugs. I hoped to gain some understanding of the psychological reasons prompting this behavior. I couldn't understand why these intelligent, well-informed college students would take a drug that posed such danger to their minds. They had many common characteristics, of which I will mention but two. First, they expressed great alienation with the adult world, especially with their families. That adults generally disapproved of the drug made its ingestion more attractive than it would otherwise be. Second, at an unusually early age, their families exerted relatively little influence on how they conducted their lives. Peer influence determined their values, their sexual behavior, and their decision to take drugs.

C. A few years ago my attention was drawn to the vast numbers of young people injured or killed on motorcycles. In the United States alone, over five thousand die each year as a result of motorcycle accidents and over a quarter million suffer serious injury. I had as patients a number of young men who had one or more of these serious accidents and I found they shared a number of characteristics that I described as the "Motorcycle Syndrome."

Publication in a medical journal brought correspondence from doctors in numerous countries, indicating that the phenomenon is worldwide. A few characteristics these motorcyclists shared were: (1) extreme passivity and inability to compete academically, athletically, or socially; (2) poor control of sexual and aggressive impulses, with anger—especially anger toward the father—turned inward, resulting in depression and a tendency to self-injury; (3) impotence and fear of being homosexual; and (4) a distant, conflict-ridden relationship with the father who was critical of and inaccessible to the boy throughout the boy's life.

D. Another research interest has been the psychological determinants of campus disorder we experienced in the United States during the past few years. I observed one such disorder as it occurred in 1969. I was struck by one fact that emerged with remarkable clarity: that the young have a peculiar sensitivity to remoteness, invisibility, and unresponsiveness on the part of adults, especially those in positions of authority. The remoteness and invisibility of the president of the university and a number of administrators alienated a large segment of the college community and seemed to parallel the remoteness and inaccessibility of parents in the childhood homes of the students.

SHIFT IN CHILD CARE

I mention briefly these impressions from my investigative and clinical work with college students because they have, in large measure, led me to an observation concerning the modern family that has far-reaching implications. I refer to the observation that in many homes today child care has shifted from parents to other agencies. A home in which both parents are available to the child, emotionally as well as physically, has become the exception rather than the rule.

And this is not the disadvantaged home where the father is missing and the mother works. I refer to even the most affluent homes.

What has been shown over and over again to have the most profound effect on the character development of a child is a close, warm relationship with *both* parents. Yet, our current mode of living makes this most difficult to attain. Many parents today relegate care of children to babysitters, to nurseries, to schools, to boarding schools, to camps, to other children, and to the television set. We have a society that is age segregated. The large family with sustained contact with grandparents, uncles, cousins, and relatives of all ages has become rare.

In an article surveying thirty different studies of child-rearing practices in the United States, over a twenty-five-year period, Bronfenbrenner of Cornell University concluded that the studies all pointed to "a progressive decrease, especially in recent decades, in the amount of contact between parents and their children." Cross-cultural studies also bear this out. United States parents spend considerably less time with their children—especially fathers—than parents in Germany and Russia. Although both Russian parents work, and although Russian children spend a great deal of time in family collectives, emotional ties between children and parents are stronger and the time spent together considerably greater than in the United States; there is relatively little juvenile delinquency in Russia. Only one country exceeds the United States in violence, crime, and delinquency and that is England. Research by Devereux et al. has shown that England is also the only country where parents spend less time with their children than those in the United States. Both parents, especially the fathers, show less affection, offer less companionship and are considerably less involved in their children's lives.

Only recently have we come to realize the full emotional impact on the child of the missing father. In the brief clinical sketches of the young people we considered, we noticed how often in their family history parents, especially fathers, were inaccessible. Many of these youth came from affluent homes, where both parents possessed a high degree of culture and education. Many suffer from what I call "the famous-father syndrome," where the father is held in awe. He is so busy providing materially for them (at least he uses this to justify his being away from home so much), that he neglects his family's emotional and spiritual needs. He may spend his time on activities that in themselves serve constructive goals. My practice is filled with the families of doctors. Who would deny that a physician's work is constructive and worthwhile? But he may be doing something good at the cost of the well-being of those he loves most. This is also true of ministers, who take care of the needs of others while the emotional needs of their families are being taken care of by psychiatrists.

You say, "All right, you have made your point. Parents perhaps are not as accessible today. But so what? Most successful professional people never have been. What hard evidence do you have that it does harm?" But let's look at where we have come.

First, in the brief glance at data from research on college youth, we note: (1) these young people suffer from some incapacitating symptomatic or characterological conflict, (2) they have in common a physically absent or an emotionally inaccessible parent, and (3) when we look at their histories carefully there appears to be some causal relationship between (1) and (2).

Second, when we consult the scientific literature we find an array of carefully controlled experiments that strongly support these impressions. The recent medical literature contains an impressive body of data that corroborates the impression that a parent's absence through death or divorce, as well as a parent's inaccessibility, either physically, emotionally, or both, exert a profound influence on an individual's emotional health or illness.

SOURCES OF WISDOM

One or two closing thoughts: It seems to me that we often run into difficulty not because of gross, obvious blunders, but because we lose perspective, our lives become somewhat out of focus, our values distorted, our priorities disordered. Sometimes a single experience can help change our perspective. During the flight of Apollo 8, we became the first people in history to see firsthand a picture of the entire earth—an awesome sphere suspended in the silence and darkness of space. I could not help but think as I viewed that picture from space that one lifetime consists of just so many rotations on that sphere. If we live to be eighty years old, we have less than thirty thousand rotations. Because we sleep about one-third of that time, the number is less than twenty thousand rotations. Can you imagine, one life equals twenty thousand spins of this globe? How incredibly few. This realization makes one want desperately to live the highest quality of life possible—with the most purpose and fulfillment. I need not tell you how far short of this goal most lives fall.

Where does one turn for wisdom in how to live this life? For an answer to basic questions of meaning and destiny, many of the best minds of the past have turned to a source we have by and large neglected today. I refer to the Old and New Testament documents. If we read these documents objectively, free of the aura of religiosity, piousness, and churchliness repugnant to all of us, we find some startling assertions and profound wisdom about how to live this life.

This wisdom is perhaps most succinctly summarized in what Christ said were the two great commandments—loving God with all of our soul and heart and mind and loving our neighbor as ourselves.

These commandments have almost become clichés today; yet, if we come close to even the most superficial understanding of them, we realize they contain more wisdom concerning this life than all the knowledge acquired by man since the beginning of time. We see immediately that they imply a new dimension to life—a spiritual dimension—without which our lives are out of focus, tilted, not quite right. Second, they make unmistakably clear what our priorities must be once we acquire this dimension. What has struck me as I have read these documents is that this Creator, whoever he is, is not at all impressed by the schools we attend, the number of degrees earned, the awards won, the papers and books written, a listing in Who's Who or in the Social Register, the amount of economic, political, or intellectual clout we wield. He appears to have one overriding concern—our relationships: first, our relationship to him; second, our relationship to others.

Our relationship to him, the first commandment says, must be characterized by love . . . Agape. Loving God necessitates knowing him, and knowing him, the New Testament says, involves an encounter with Christ, an encounter that transforms our lives and brings the purpose of our lives into clear focus. The Old and New Testament documents, it seems to me, all point clearly to the three most significant events in human history that make this encounter with Christ possible, namely, his birth, his death, and His resurrection.

Our relationship with others brings us to the second commandment and to our second priority—of loving our neighbor. And this in turn brings us to where we started, to the family. Who is our neighbor? Christ, when asked this, told the story of the good Samaritan, implying our neighbor is the first person we come across in need. And doesn't that include, first and foremost, our family, those who share our home? I think so.

If we are even to begin to live the few days we have been given on this earth with any sense of fulfillment and joy, we must begin to give thought and effort to our relationships to God, family, and work in that order. When these priorities are out of order, when we give first place to what ought to be third place, we may be very successful—for a while. But then our spiritual life—if we have any—begins to deteriorate, then our family relationships, then everything else. But when we put first things first, second and third things don't decrease, as we fear, but actually increase. That's a principle that runs throughout life. The Scriptures state it this way, "Seek ye first the kingdom of God and his righteousness and all these things will be added."

Part III

PARADOXICAL HOPE

. . . God is at work in you, both to will and to
work for his good pleasure.

PHILIPPIANS 2:13

Reconciliation to God is reconciliation to life itself; love to the Creator is love of being, rejoicing in existence, in its source, totality and particularity. . . . Love to God is conviction that
there is faithfulness at the heart of things:
unity, reason, form and meaning in the plural-
ity of being.

H. RICHARD NIEBUHR,
The Purpose of the Church
and Its Ministry

OVERVIEW

The preceding five chapters highlight many edges in life where the Christian laity is challenged to creative witness and service. I would not, however, want the specifics of our sociological and historical situation to overshadow the overarching theme of paradoxical Christian hope intersecting despair. It is fitting in the overview of this third and final section to reflect briefly on part II.

Hope for the home is hope for the nation; the morality of big structures, be they nations or corporations, depend on the morality of the smaller units comprising them; our moral vision for the nation depends on personal perceptions of morality. All Christian hope is paradoxical. It says "no" to the world when the world tries to lay first claim on love and commitment; it says "yes" to the world when God and divine righteousness are first in love and commitment.

The Great Commandment quoted by Armand Nicholi in chapter 10 has two prongs, love transcendent for God and love immanent for humanity, which must be kept in balance in personal and ecclesiastical life. Personal faith split from social application is theological schizophrenia—one without the other is deformed and deforming. Parodists of the Christian faith have made sport of our divisions, enjoyed our family feud. In a simpler generation, they had great fun splitting the Christian vision into the dirty here and now and the sweet by and by. We masochistically joined in. Evangelicals "so heavenly minded they were no earthly good" pitted against the liberal activists, "eyes fastened to the earth, missing the stars." Today, however, I believe the old stereotypes are falling away. I see a new Christian synthesis emerging, confounding the critics with its will toward unity.

C. S. Lewis says in *Mere Christianity* that Christian focus on the eternal world is not, as some modern persons think, "a form of escapism or wishful thinking, but one of the things a Christian is meant to do. It does not mean that we are to leave the present world as it is." People whose minds are occupied with heaven, Lewis writes, have a way of leaving their mark on earth more effectively than those preoccupied with the earth: "Aim at Heaven and you will get Earth 'thrown in': aim at Earth and you will get neither."

The laity lives at the edge of hope, where the Cross intersects with despair. The laity lives at the edge of the church where resurrection intersects with the world. With despair there is no paradox, only flat, monotonous sameness, boredom and death; by contrast, hope sparkles with the many-splendored diversity of life's facets, dancing its pluralistic dance in the spotlight of eternity's mirrored ballroom. For the hope-centered laity, life at the edges cannot be repressed; in the darkest night it is forever breaking out, kicking up its heels in anticipated and unanticipated joy.

The Christian laity is called to *do,* but more important, and prerequisite, is the call to *be.* Christian witnessing is not essentially anything we do; witnesses is what we are. Christian *being* in paradoxical hope is human creativity, and just as the Divine Creativity incarnates itself in our Lord, it expresses itself, by the Spirit, in our human flesh. In the world of sameness Eugene Kennedy calls "plastic," in the world of animality James Reston calls a "pigsty," in a world of pride Malcolm Muggeridge calls "buffoonery," the creativity of hope comes as a cool, welcome breeze. Hell, it occurs to me, is buffoonery in plastic pigstys, and all us prodigals know the taste of "the husks that the swine would eat." Miraculously, in the Triune God we need not remain prodigal, but through redeeming love can become God's men and women—unique, spontaneous human beings potentially loving, truthful, peacemaking, fearless, gentle, therapeutic, joyful: all the things I, and we, too often are not! Despite repetitive shortfallings, the Christian finds it impossible to give up the hope of achieving what Oswald Chambers calls "calm, quiet sanity" in life and what Thomas a Kempis called "the Imitation of Christ," which is the fully mature creativity of Christian character.

Creativity is too often thought of in terms of the arts, too infrequently thought of as love in our relationships. We think of creative science, but not of creative morality. Artists, writers, actors, dancers, and designers of spaceships are creative. It also takes creativity to manage a hospital, communicate with a child or parent, teach the ABC's, cook a good meal, or try to be moral in the world. (Chambers says the work of the Spirit within us is "moral originality.") It takes creativity to be a Christian. And it takes the combined gifts of all Christians to evangelize, to demonstrate reconciliation, to bind up the world's wounds: group creativity. It takes faith to be creative at the edge of hope; faith that Christ's ultimate creativity is within us; faith to believe we are, as Colossians says, "complete in him." Moving as many of us do at great speed to either fulfill or escape the "work ethic," it takes faith to slow down, take time, and concentrate on the creativity of *being*.

Hope within us is itself creative. It lifts us from remorse, dispels fears, brightens our integrity and sends us on to live confidently in the imperfect world, pinioned between promise and fulfillment. To me, the two following chapters are exercises in creative hope. Neither explores hope as a category of formal theology. Rather, the first, "Risking Creativity," shows a group of Christians at the Congress of the Laity struggling together to understand the source and the forms of the creativity required in serving God and humanity. The second, "The Immanent Christ and Human Creativity," broadens the perspective of all who hope in Christ. It sharpens the Christian's eye for seeing God and human worldly responsibility in the light of wholeness. It links the paradox of hope with creativity.

Part III is, in a real sense, the Martin Marty part of this book. Chapter twelve, the last chapter, is a text Marty prepared for Sunday morning at the congress. His reading was accompanied by scores of slides depicting the world in which we live and our human aspirations as those are captured by artists. The script, however, is quite independent of any graphic accompaniment. Its style and verbal images naturally paint pictures in the reader's mind, and the text has been edited in only minor ways for publication.

"Risking Creativity," chapter 11, is drawn from a congress workshop led by Marty. I have selected long verbatim episodes from the proceedings because, it seems to me, the format and content get very close to the heart of the Congress of the Laity. In what both Marty and the seminar participants say, I find amplification of the congress' purpose and illustration of the value of Christians from diverse backgrounds together exploring the meaning of faith. At the end of the chapter, I have briefly noted several themes that merit continuing dialogue among lay Christians. Each of these, in its own way reflecting despairs we all have felt, throws added light on the theme, the creativity of paradoxical hope.

Chapter Eleven

RISKING CREATIVITY

Martin Marty entitled his workshop at the Congress of the Laity, "Do-It-Yourself Creativity Kit: Religious Resources for Secular Life." There is something a little tongue in cheek about the title, as Marty told the group in a section not quoted below. Kenneth Wilson, the former editor of *Christian Herald* magazine, says he feels it is important to have a sense of humor in matters religious, to have "fun" with one's faith. I agree, and so does Marty. He pointed out that he often writes columns "chuckling about all the things offered by way of 'how to' and 'do it yourself'—more than forty pages of *Books in Print* are filled with titles starting with 'How to.' You just can't imagine the number of things there, but the closer they get to the personality, the more likely they are to overoffer—to suggest too much you can do on your own." Said Marty, "Christians need to remind the world that human creativity, our 'how to,' has a source—God."

In our earthly sphere, people are creative. We see creativity everyday, everywhere. And in the service of the Lord, the Christian laity must risk individual and corporate creativity—take creative risks, and I would say the church as an institution must do the same. Marty and his group went considerably beyond the two hours alloted for the workshop in their quest for what it means to be creative as a Christian. Only part of the proceedings are printed here. The first hour was devoted to an exercise that Marty called "a trigger for a process." Individuals responded on paper to eight questions then shared around. In order to supply context, the eight questions are given, and the dialogue picks up with the discussion of the last two. Marty's questions were:

——Who, to you, is the most creative living person in your line of work?

——How do you account for that person's spark?

——From the creative point of view, if you couldn't be yourself, who that is presently living would you like to be?

——Who from the past would you most like to be?

——Think of yourself, when are you most creative—time of week, time of year?

——Is there a special setting in which you are most creative?

——Is there anything in the faith—a doctrine, a symbol, a mood, an event—which gives impetus to your creativity?

——Is there anything in the faith that holds back your creativity?

(In the following conversation, progressive sections are marked by group leader comments or questions signaled by the name *Marty*. Other remarks by Marty are designated *MM*. The asterisk (*) indicates a seminar participant is speaking. In few cases does it matter whether successive voices are the same or different, and in those instances where it matters the context indicates a difference.)

MARTIN MARTY: What in the faith sparks (creativity)?

* Hymns.

MM Ah, yes. My father was a church organist. I walk into a church on Saturday afternoon when the organist is practicing and that's when I can really get my pad out and think.

* Prayer.

MM Probably a great underutilized form in connection with creativity. We usually think of prayer as a set-aside time, routinized or panic time, but if it is true that human creativity is involved in divine creativity there is no way to get there except prayer.

* Praise.

* Watching Jesus in the Gospels . . . the creative interrelations.

* The parable of the talents.

* The vision of the Bible; it's forward-looking, visionary, involved in risk-taking.

MM One of the great atheists of our time, Ernst Bloch, a Marxist maverick of East Germany, speaks in those terms. He says the Bible is an infatuation with the possible . . . God is ahead of us.

* Innovation of hope.

MM The faith doesn't only talk about the future, it projects us into it.

* Consciousness of *corum deum* . . .

MM "In the presence . . ." The medievals thought of the relationship to God in two ways—*vertus deum,* over against God, and *corum deum,* in the presence of God. It's a liberating thought for creativity. My mentor, Martin Luther, when he was in agony, went to his confessor, "How do I know I'm saved?" The confessor said, "Well, you can't know what's going on in the mind of God but you can see the wounds of Christ."

* Obligation to serve others.

* The sermon on Sunday morning, when it's good.

MM You know what makes a sermon good?

* Creative listening.

MM You're right.

* The Holy Spirit, especially when I've agreed to take a job at church I really can't do, then I have an idea I don't think came from me at all.

* Standing on "son-ship rights."

MM What we are seeing in what we are saying is that if we are free to be creative in a religious sense there has to be a sense of open connection. As long as we are self-preoccupied—"How'm I doing God?" it doesn't happen.

[177]

* Prophetic voices.

MM "Make the way of the Lord."

* The universality of sin, which makes it all right to fail.

MM Yeah, sin is useful in a lot of ways. It dispells illusions.
. . . Having to feel a cause is good only if you're winning
is the death of creativity.

* The continuum of life.

MARTY: Okay. What in the faith holds us back?

* Guilt.

* Unconfessed sin.

* Doubt.

* Fear.

* Pride.

* Organizational structures of the church.

* Not knowing God's specific message to you.

MM Knowing something is out there but not knowing what it
is trying to say.

* Apathy.

* Inadequate role for women in the church.

MM Not many of these things are integral to the faith, are
they? The faith is designed to help us get rid of these. I
think the faith is out to get a different role for women in
the church, and I don't think the faith implies a heavy organizational structure, and we know it is supposed to
address unconfessed sins and guilt. The church does bring
us into an orbit where these things have to be wrestled
with—What else?

* When answers come too completely and concisely.

MM You mean, when they are too concise, they stop creativity?

* Right.

* Dogmatism.

* Perfectionism.

MM We seem to have a pattern going on in these. Dogma, fine; dogmatism, problem—premature closures. Did you ever stop to think about it, the two biggest questions in the Bible are not answered. They are lived. God is never satisfactorily brought on stage for us to check him out, and evil is never philosophically done away with. Evil is regularly addressed but Jesus lived out the circumstances.

. . . .

MARTY: Here's a picture of a wheelbarrow done by Edward De Bono. What's wrong with it?

* The handles are where the wheels should be.

* It's too short.

* Too deep.

* There's no leverage.

MM Did you think of what I did to mess up the creative case of this wheelbarrow by the question I asked? I asked, "What's wrong with it?" and you were nice enough to play my game. But what if I asked, "What's interesting about it." De Bono showed the wheelbarrow to some children, and here are four things they told him. One said, "Hey, that's interesting." A little child working with it would be close enough, if you get mud on the wheel, to kick it off. Second one said, "That's neat, because if you come up to a pit, the wheel would stay on top and you could just tip it over." The third one had an idea for a trapdoor with a string, pull the string to unload; and the fourth proposed a window with a piston and spring inside, a gauge with red and green lights so you could keep filling as long as the light stays green. De Bono is not saying it's a good wheelbarrow. He's saying watch out what the question is. . . . Think how often in our church or your firm or your family an issue isn't addressed until it is in bad shape or there's a crisis situation, then you ask, "What's wrong?" If you start by asking, "What's interesting?" I think you get off on a much different tract. Of course, you can't always do that. Some of the issues in our society are so drastic, the people so polarized in advance, that it is hard to get creative.

I like those issues the church still has a chance to address before society makes up its mind. One that I spent some time on with friends in the pastorate four or five or six years ago was amnesty for deserters and draft dodgers in the Vietnam war. I say this is a kind of luxurious one because all the arguments on either side can be addressed fairly evenly and it's not the one people on either side thought would make the republic fall apart, whichever way it was solved. But it's an important issue, an indicative and symbolic issue. I found it interesting because I was right in the middle and so think I could hear both points of view. We discovered that if you do not prepare a group ahead of time it will not think creatively on an issue like amnesty. The people will bring something from the outside. . . . In several debates I heard in congregations and church circles, neither side ever evoked anything from the Word of God or their tradition or their theology. . . .

I found it more creative when the question on amnesty wasn't "what's wrong?" but "what's interesting?" It was interesting to try to prepare a group in advance, to make some agreements. First, both sides agree not to break the fellowship over the issue. . . . Second, say what's on their minds on the premises. . . . Third, both sides have to listen to the other wrestling with the issue in terms of its vision of the Word of God, the tradition of the church, or theology. . . . I'm not saying that changed the nation. I don't think we have real resolutions to a lot of issues, but asking "what's interesting?" did produce freedom for a kind of thinking we didn't have before and, since there are so many issues today, we have a lot of chances. Pius XII once said, "We should thank God he has placed us in the middle of so many problems it is no longer permitted us to be mediocre."

MARTY: Let's work on the definition of creativity. What is it?

* Bringing into being something that never existed before.

MM Good start. Always something innovative or novel about creativity. If the world were already here and God just reproduced it we wouldn't call that creation. It need not be wholly new but at least a new combination. I think we underestimate the extent to which Christian resources have something to do with creation. . . . We are to continue creation. We are the people who put the next connection together. The dazzling freedom to do that, but it's grounded in a view of the divine Creator, and I think that's liberating.

. . . .

* The end result of a lot of conditions, some conscious, some not.

MM Aren't we talking process? What is creativity itself?

* Allowing persons to share something happening deep within them.

MM You'd see the personal dimension, not the "it" world?

* Expression of personality.

* Inspiration.

* Bringing into existence something that already exists in the mind of God.

MM That would be the use of the divine prototype.

* Seeing something in, say, a block of marble, that exists in your own mind.

MM . . . I can tell you exactly how to create a great statue, say, of an elephant, out of a block of marble. . . . You get a big block of marble and chip away everything that doesn't look like an elephant!

. . . .

MM We're dealing in our definition-making to this point with latencies in the mind of God and human raw material. What else is creativity?

* Revelation.

MM Unpack that a bit.

* You see something coming out of something . . . a creative idea out of something thousands have seen before but never saw what you see.

MM That's a big part of creation, isn't it? Churchill said you can hear something a thousand times and the thousand and first time, it's true; suddenly hits.

* Finding a connection between what is interesting in one person's experience and what I think is interesting in mine.

MM As long as it's not random. Definitions of creativity don't usually allow for the random. They come down to comprehensibility and understandability. Creation is not normally luck, even if it has revelation, inspiration, and the other qualities we have named. At the Second City in Chicago they were saying once, certainly it's possible for a monkey with a typwriter and an infinite amount of time to eventually type out "Hamlet." Somebody proposed that an infinite number of monkeys could do it instantaneously. But we don't call that creation, if it's luck or random.

. . . .

* Visions or a dream. I'm thinking of the civil rights movement, which was created out of a dream.

MM In social movements, it almost always goes this way: There is a generalized discontent, a generalized thought that something ought to be better, then along comes what I called "horizonal people"—they get to the horizon first and already see what others do not see yet. That's real creative art. . . .

* I try to tell adolescents when I give them writing assignments, creativity is a matter of seeing what isn't there.

* I'm concerned. Here we have eight hundred supposedly creative persons at this congress. . . . Aren't we, as Christians, responsible for helping other people develop their creative potential. . . . I haven't sensed that in the discussion here.

MM How do you get from one to the other?

* I'm not sure, but I think we ought to be concerned about it.

MM Isn't there a tremendous ripple effect? You can't start with the whole. Societies don't move because everyone gets to the same place at the same time in the same way. In almost every movement, there are certain people, and they don't have to be smarter or richer, who have a catalytic effect because they're in a certain circumstance—Rosa Parks on the bus in Montgomery, somebody mixing up chemicals and noticing something different. . . . Don't underestimate what eight hundred people could do. Jesus of Nazareth spent his whole ministry on twelve people in order to save all the Americans. But I like your point. We shouldn't think there should be only privileged places where we discuss creativity for its own sake.

. . . .

MARTY: Creativity, its features. We tend to call something creative if it is new, a discovery, has positive effect, is discerning. That is one set of definitions. It is comprehensible as opposed to the random, and orders an existence somehow or other. If you don't misinterpret this word, I think creation has a "useful" context. By "useful" I don't mean pragmatic, grim, productive. . . . Dance is not useful in the sense of getting the dishes washed, but its design is to delight and in that sense it's useful. [In creativity], we get away from the random, yet creation is born of putting together a lot of things we never thought to put together before.

* I have a feeling we are constantly being deluded in thinking anyone is capable of original creation. Isn't all we're doing reordering, rediscovering, innovating with what the Creator has made? Is that too much [to say]?

MM Not too much if it's designed to keep us in our place. . . . The death of creativity is . . . the Promethian—we

seized the fire from the gods and we're going to use it.
What I would resist is the idea that is has all been done
before. I think our Creator placed in this world an infinite
number of possibilities. I think we have to see what all
hasn't been connected yet. I want to take very seriously
what you said because in our world creation is ordinarily
divorced from its ground in the Creator. . . .

My theologian in America is Jonathan Edwards . . .
who said life should be called "consent to being." God is
already there—we have erected the barriers—and life is a
"consent to being" out of which all relationships are created. Edwards couldn't pose "reason" versus "emotion."
They couldn't finally be in contradiction. . . . Edwards
said reason and "affection" [his word for "emotion"] have
to be grounded in Being Itself—God. . . . If your reason
is grounded in the divine Creator and you stay in touch
with that, there are just an infinite number of possibilities
open to you. . . .

* In this context, I think the real inspiration and challenge is
the partnership with our Creator. When parents produce
a child, I think this is participating in the creation of our
God, on-going creation. I think there are all kinds of possibilities for being creative when our source is the Creator.

MM The source is what we're really on right now. If our life
is transparent to the Creator, then we don't worry about
the outcome. It's when lives get opaque that we worry.

* To be creative is to tap God's creative flow, which is already there.

MM We're on a very important point here. . . . I don't think
the Christian church has any reason to claim monopolies
on social justice, beauty, or managerial skill. Luther once
said, "Better to be governed by a smart Turk than a dumb
Christian.". . . . But if we're going to be a witness in the
world, we should be the ones who constantly remind the
world of this transparency to the Creator.

* I wrote down, the Creator created and gave us the ability
to take what he gave us and become creative ourselves.

MM. . . . So many of our words keep reminding us that the Christian faith is one of hope and new connection.

* Isn't that the role of the Holy Spirit in the Christian? Of myself, I cannot please God. This is all through Scripture, that God, through the Spirit, whom I have the moment I receive Jesus Christ, is now in control. And this subtle business of Romans where Paul talks about the sin-nature and the Spirit. . . . When the Spirit is in control, God is acting through me. When I'm in control, I can shut out the Spirit. He doesn't leave me but I shut him off. This is the eternal struggle of the Christian. The make-believe Christian doesn't have the struggle because he doesn't even have the Spirit, hence the whole problem of the true Christian versus make-believe Christian, who has fooled himself because he doesn't have the power of the Spirit of God in him.

* That's an arrogant statement. I really think it's an affront for you to assume there are "make-believe" Christians. Maybe for you to turn yourself over to the power of God is where you are, but for you to say there are "make-believe" Christians is an inappropriate statement.

MM Let's keep this alive. This is very useful. . . .

* I think of us all being created in God's image. Therefore, the creative force in us is in God's image.

* In my mind, God is not a fixed being. . . .

MM I may need help to bail us out here. Let me first say what I like and then where I have trouble [with the statement on the Spirit]. I like the connection of creation and Spirit—*creator* and *spiritus*—which is too often forgotten. When we talk in clearly trinitarian terms we sometimes get the sense that creation is God's acting way back then . . . and that's it. In classical Christian theology . . . *creator-spiritus* is initiating activity. He is enlightening us: the fire of the Spirit. What I would call into question is not so much the judgment as the verb. I'm always nervous about "having" the Spirit. I think that suggests that God is, in a

[185]

sense, possessable. He *has* me but I don't *have* him. I sense that the Spirit is a torrent, a flow, and all the words of having and possessing—and I know there are places in the Bible where you get right into the orbit of such words a little—make me nervous. Spirit is an eruptive way of talking about the God you can't control or grasp.

* St. John says it beautifully in his First Epistle—We would be incapable of loving anyone unless God had first loved us. . . . [Yet] people who don't know God can still love, they experience him even though they don't know him. I think the same applies with creation, Spirit and Creator, all of it together. God has us. Do we know God has us?. . . . In everything that is created, somehow God is present there, but through conversion we become aware ourselves that God has us.

MM . . . . I think that in the arts, in management, in government, in homemaking, or wherever, we're interested not in confining the Spirit but in witnessing to it where Spirit comes.

* Karl Rahner has said, if we really believe that the salvation brought by Jesus to the world is as powerful as the sin of Adam on the world, if we really believe that, giving God to a person is not pouring God onto that person but drawing God out. . . .

MM Karl Barth's version of that is to ask why we always look at each other in Adam instead of in Christ.

* I'm wondering what part friction plays in creativity. . . . I hadn't before felt the aliveness created in this room by the two conflicting views [on the phrase "make-believe" Christian]. I'm grateful to both persons. I expect a lot of us, I know I did, immediately began to ask where we stand on the matter and all kinds of creative thought processes started. My level of thinking was raised.

The conversation continued along these same basic lines. That person who introduced the matter of "having" the

Spirit had opportunity to defend himself on the strength of Romans 8 and there were degrees of agreement and further disagreement. "Agony" as a dimension of creativity was brought up, and there was discussion of semantics—all very interesting, but enough has been quoted to grasp the thrust and to pinpoint several concerns I believe the Christian laity need bear in mind as we seek unity, maturity and engagement.

1. Views do conflict, on interpretation of Scripture, understanding of doctrines and church practice, and on social application of the Gospel. Let us not pretend they do not, but I want to link the reality of difference to the point Marty made in recalling his experience with congregations debating amnesty. Our unity in love may never extend to slants on the Scripture, to doctrine and practice, but we can most certainly shore up the love by agreeing to not let disagreement disrupt Christian fellowship. And our fellowship can only be strengthened by speaking honestly to one another and listening to the other side on an issue as it interacts with the Word of God and our theology.

Nothing is uglier, more distasteful, than situations in which people sit politely silent in church meetings or theological conversations, sit not expressing disagreement, then go out and talk behind the backs of others—not caring enough to argue. We ought to speak up, say what is on our minds. And there is a time for listening, really listening to others. Head-nodding may not always be listening because sometimes we are trying to think of the next clever thing we will say. Sometimes silence is appropriate, sometimes talk. A reporter at the Congress of the Laity heard the person sitting behind him say to a friend, "You know, this whole meeting is great but not because I agree with everything I've heard. It's—well, time was when I would hear one speaker and say, 'ah, yeah, that's right.' Then another speaker would say something entirely different and I'd say, 'Yeah, that's right.' And I didn't know what I thought. Now, over the past few years, I've tried to think about what I believe, so that when I hear these speakers here I at least know whether I agree or disagree, and maybe one of them will change my mind, but I'll know it's changing." Bravo for that kind of growth. All of us find out what we think by a combination of using our minds and listening to others, disciplining ourselves inwardly and outwardly.

2. Marty used the phrase "hope and new connection." That is exciting. There are so many new connections the laity can make in hope, connections among ourselves across the dividing lines of denomination, race, and theology; connections between clergy and laity; and connections between the faith and the issues of our world. A fair number of connections have already been made with social problems. Human rights, poverty, ecology, public morality, and others have been identified within religion's interests. But so little has yet been done by the laity to connect faith to medical ethics, psychiatry, economic theory, labor-management relations, foreign policy, and organizational life.

3. The "ripple effect" is extremely important in spreading enthusiasm for lay Christian initiatives in secular society. I do not personally believe that the clergy should be asked to or can lead a lay awakening. The leadership must come from the laity itself as we rub shoulders in all those places where we come in contact. Laity under God, decentralized, diversified, dispersed, with professional leadership in the servant role, pastoral authority in the body as a whole: this is the secret. The original Christian community numbered a few more than twelve, but it was small, and that little band of disciples could not have started the process of taking the Gospel to the uttermost parts by working only among themselves. These folks, laity all, since they were not Jewish priests, and ordination as we know it had not been invented; these followers of the Lord risked losing everything, including their group security, by moving out in many directions. How audacious for Peter and John to testify in faith before rulers, of Paul to preach in Athens! Have we no audacity in saying to our colleagues of the laity, "We have a responsibility in this world. Let us proceed, each in his own place but also all together!"?

4. "The God we do not control," someone in the workshop session said. Mighty words for us to hear and believe.

Given my experience and vocabulary, it troubles me not at all to speak of "having" the Holy Spirit in my heart because, in that usage, "having" implies presence. I "have" a wife. That is a fact. I know no other verb to use, but I assuredly do not "possess" or "own" her. Good grief, no! And never, never do we, human beings, have Christ in our clutches— God in a box. This is an especially important truth to realize in times of religious revival. Among Christians, boosterism should always be tempered by an acute awareness of sin— our own.

5. "Having to feel a cause is good only if you're winning is the death of creativity," Marty said. I like that. His words apply, for me, to the cause of lay awakening. On the scoreboard on which our present culture counts points, we could hardly say we are winning. Someone has said, "I'd rather fail in a cause that will ultimately succeed than succeed in one that will fail."

I believe in the potential of the laity to change our society, to bring healing to it before it self-destructs, but as the paradox of the debate opening this book suggests, people like Malcolm Muggeridge who love God more than they love our civilization are essential to fulfill Peter Berger's hope, and the hope of many others, for its improvement and salvation. Will Western civilization survive its present crises? No doubt, if it turns to God, it could; the biblical promises are clear. But will it happen; will it turn? I do not know, although I firmly believe God's will shall ultimately prevail. Ultimately, of course, it does not matter whether either Western civilization or the cause of lay awakening "wins" or "loses." What matters is our Christian obedience, doing God's will daily. That, as Marty says, is creativity; that, viewed in transcendence and immanence, is victory.

Chapter Twelve

THE IMMANENT CHRIST AND HUMAN CREATIVITY

Martin E. Marty

You create.

Your hands, your body, your mind are the instruments you use.

In doing so, you continue the creating work of God. In ways that you seldom consider, this work comes to focus in Jesus Christ. In Paul's letter to the Colossians, 1:15–18 (NEB, RSV), we hear the astonishing word that "in Christ everything in heaven and on earth was created. . . . and in him all things hold together."

It does not look that way. The world seems to be "on its own." It does not seem to "hold together." You need different eyes to see that it does. This . . . biblical study is an exercise in a different way of seeing.

Fold and flex your hands, look at them, think about them, watch hands being creative.

We look in seven directions:

1. The artist reshapes the raw material of earth, clay, or pigment not of her making.
2. Music comes from the sounds of creation, and our hands on keys or strings shape it.
3. The flow of ideas from the mind of the writer to the eye of the reader comes through hands holding quills or typing.

Not all creativity is artistic:

4. Humans create their cities and govern them when they mark their ballots or pull voting-machine levers or push doorbells for politics.
5. In their professions, gifted hands of surgeons continue life where they do not create it.
6. In public service and welfare it is the hand stretched out in help or love that creates new opportunity.
7. In business, people make their point through gesture, through reach, through direction.

You "see" all this everyday. Most people most days go about their ways unconscious of the divine source. Take a second look in the same seven directions; it is obvious that the act of creating can go wrong, can turn demonic. Thus visual arts lose their source and become violent, vulgar, assaulting. Musicians outdo each other in efforts to shock and depict the ugly. You look at your friendly neighborhood newsstand and wonder what Paul ever meant when he said that "all things hold together" in Christ. They do not hold together at all: Where is the common theme? In government, the mannequins of state who scheme astutely to blot each other's names from the pages of history shape weapons and show power far from any roots in Christ.

When have the headlines last suggested that the professions "hold together" through his power and love?

Use your ordinary eyes and ordinary way of looking, and see the city, its neighborhoods, its poor and desperate people—will you find foretastes of a new Jerusalem? Do eyes show human dealings that find something of the divine image in the human world? The eyes have their own answers; all we need are images to stimulate them.

Now, the worst thing we could do in putting on the new spectacles is to look for a creative God and a coherence in Christ only under their visible signs. You walk into a gallery and see something of the boldness and grandeur, the sweep of line, the "holy emptiness" created by light—but miss the Jesus of Sunday school art and fail to "see" creation. Your child guitars a folk tune, the madrigal group sings a madrigal, the symphony plays its overture, and you do not hear the divine source, because you do not hear the Sunday words of hymns. You can wear blinders and be parochial, missing the divine way in the human library by failing to see that God can work in books that do not deal directly with his word.

You look further, in the public sphere. Certainly legislatures and courts, whether in our country or serving many countries, are not churches and their halls do not look like sanctuaries. So you can easily miss the point that when they "talk, talk" instead of "kill, kill," they let shine through something of the Christ in whom life coheres. You find yourself in conventions that are not Eucharistic congresses or evangelistic rallies and find it easy to overlook the activity of a God who does not shelter himself around altars and pulpits, is not lead-encased in congregations.

As for the human city, do you see life? "You can kill a person with an apartment as easily as with a gun—it only takes a little longer." But behind the rows of windows are lives, each of them open to creative acts that the Christian must say find their source in God. And when your eyes scan the symbols of human power, you must see that our cities can be signs of Babylon or Jerusalem, that they are "beguiling to beasts and infants alike," that "hell is a city much like London" but that heaven breaks through the images of the earthly city.

Now that your eye is trained to do its searching and sorting we are ready to move into a sphere in which "creativity" and "Christ" link more obviously. If you look, you will find in past and present the evidences that artists' hands respond to the imaging of Jesus Christ in the middle of our world. Far from the world of punk rock is the "divine elemental roar of the organ," which reaches into the depths of the soil for its undertone and aspires to heavens with its flute stops, with sound designed to connote coherence in Christ. In our day, as more obviously in the long ago, some writers' hands shape words into passages that cause us to be "surprised by joy" in the Christian sense, at the edge of the sanctuary.

Once more, do not confine Christian creativity to the arts and letters. You find it when people in public life "press the flesh" and work out the compromises by which governments progress. In partisan life, it may be hard to see the divine imaging "across the aisle." See Christian response not only during the minute of prayer when the chaplain visits at the start of day; stay around to see men and women of conscience wrestle with issues of good and evil, justice and lawlessness as the day goes on. Why do people set aside some academies of higher learning, there to converge on sciences and arts in the name of Christ—if they did not seek to find him immanent in the middle of their world?

While Christians claim no monopoly on works of love and welfare, they do not abdicate from the "helping industries," creating agencies through which they show that they still see Christ in the neighbor in need. And even in the busy world of business and professions they set aside lodges and retreats where Christians can "come out of hiding" from the public world, "go into hiding" around the Word, and then, after retreat and quiet, advance again into the streets and jungles of modern interaction—carrying something of the freshly glimpsed Christ with them. They must believe he is present, not only at that retreat but also in the world to which they return.

You can see that the ways we act suggest that we want to see the world in a new way, to see Christ in the middle of it. How he comes, how he greets us, how we find him—those are the issues, now, as when Paul wrote. He wrote to Christians at Colossae, people who, like we, do not have the world to ourselves in cozy retreats. Now, as then, it is possible for us to get the corrections between the divine and human, the transcedent and the immanent wrong.

Animism is one way that Paul would have us reject. He did not regard everything around him as openly, completely spiritual and sacred, as if all matter pulsed with divine life. No, the world also contained the demonic; the created world "groaned," awaiting redemption. Then, as now, one could walk a street and find a shelf full of deities, an avenue of altars, but Paul knew polytheism, the idea of "many gods," only diverted the searcher. "Gods there be many, and lords there by many, but for us there is one Lord, Jesus Christ," he wrote for his community and ours.

In the days of the Colossians there were many who looked

at the mountains and lakes, the trees and the soil, and equated them with God, pantheists who saw nothing natural that they refused to call God, and such distractors blur our vision now as then.

Perhaps the full idea of God as an impersonal watchmaker, who sets in motion processes and then disappears, was a later invention, but this "deist" way that saw order without divine Person had advocates already then, and they almost dominate now.

And, when Paul wrote, some already stood around and stared at those processes and lost all sense of a creator behind them. Today, amid the tubes of our laboratories and computers of our social science centers, a new dogma reigns: We are "nothing but" atoms and molecules and behavioral response systems. This atheist way never occured to Paul.

Yet animism, polytheism, pantheism, deism, and atheism are not the real temptations for Christians.

Our first temptation is to celebrate "transcendence without immanence," to sing of a God who is so much beyond us that we do not see Him or his Christ *at all* beyond the immediate Word or outside the sanctuary. In this song, he is too "pure" to touch our world; he belongs only to the realm of heavens, clouds, angels, or among the huddles of humans who never really let him touch their common lives.

At the opposite extreme, we celebrate "immanence without transcendence," as if Christ belonged wholly to the smorgasbord of earthly sights and delights, tastes and sensations, as if there were no distance at all between the things I like and the giver.

Today we can get perspective on the world as a little blue globe. It looks self contained. We can claim that in it one person somehow rose above us, a "man for others," a good teacher and a generous human—and forget entirely Paul's words that Christ "is the image of the invisible God," (Col. 1:15) and that he "invades" our realm from the depths of the divine Being, from what is "beyond" us (Col. 1:16). Then, when the earthly delights and the perspective of order disappear, we think he is gone because in the garbage and junk of human affairs he is hard to find. The debris of human messings-up at least serves to refute those who simply want to find Christ and the world as one.

Paul wrote because the Colossians wanted to take a third way to connect the beyond and the here, the transcendent and the immanent. Their congregation was plagued with people who looked for signs and omens, who built ladders of connection between divine and human and crowded them with hierarchies of angels and demons, steps and stages. And they have not disappeared from us, either.

I suggest that a fourth division is our problem. Call it "compartmentalization," and remember that it is the great problem for the Christian laity. We box a transcendent God in his category and box ourselves in our own. Look and see whether this is your problem. Let us once again make our seven symbolic "stops."

In the arts we know as Christians how to recognize Sunday art, sacred art, transcendent themes—and then walk away and have "other-six-days" art which we think is abandoned and by itself. The choir in church, that is the easy place to hear the transcendent theme, even if often offkey and then when we close the church doors we abandon to itself the musical world, letting its sounds corrupt and asking no questions of its intent and achievement. So long as the cadences of King James and his version surround us, so long as the candle glow falls on its pages, we know what "inspiration" means. But after the hour of Scripture we move from one box, in which we have shut up God, into other categories, caring not at all what ideas shape the world. Then we fault the world for being secular—with as much right as blond parents fault their child for being blond—we produced it!

In the public realm the drawing of lines and creating of boxes is even more obvious. In the confines of the prayer breakfast, where in a windowless world, poised above oatmeal and surrounded by our kind, we create prayers, we feel spiritually at home. But do we rejoice when people carry their prayer life and light into the sector where no one gives Christians their quarter or space, and where they do not listen for and should not expect direct "witness"?

The compartmentalist who keeps apart the "divine" and

the "image" knows that the transcendent belongs in the zone between pulpit and pew and the immanent between law and citizen, or between medical text and body or textbook and student—zones we know not how to interrupt or interpret in Christ. Transcendent-minded Christians can huddle in Sunday School classes, at masses, or in retreats, and stop seeing Christ immanent where he equally announced his presence, among the alone and the needy and in the lives that stretch and stoop to meet the needs. Not for a minute do we underestimate the value of the bent knee, the folded hand, the minute "apart," but the new spectacles have to connect the divine working *somehow* with the world of boardroom and market.

That *somehow* of connection is clear for Paul and will be clear for us if we get the story right from the beginning. This is "Bible study" of a different sort, an act of seeing that searches for the immanent Christ in human creativity. But if our form is different, the story has to be the same. The Christian plot sees the point of contact in what we call "Incarnation." The "image of the invisible God" appears not in power but in weakness, not in riches but in poverty, not in pomp but as a gurgling, burping, swaddled, helpless child—the first clue that he will be immanent in unexpected places. The Gospel of John says that the divine Word "tented" among us, planted his tipi among us nomads and exiles. And when we find him, we hear Paul say that in this tenter, "the complete being of God, by God's own choice, came to dwell."

Paul, our teacher here, was found by God on a road one day, and followed that road wherever God led him. He wrote the Colossians from prison, a natural habitat for many of the most creative and courageous followers of the way of the Cross. He never found Christ disappearing when the prison shut on him, did not find Christ locked out of his heart when he wrote his famous prison letters. But the bars and chains were confining and frustrating spiritually, for they kept Paul from the new converts.

That is why he left letters and lessons, for he addressed timeless confusions of Christians. Paul warned against those who thought God was to be found in the desert, if only they who went there fasted enough and scourged themselves enough. He had to fight off those who equated God with governmental ritual and trappings of power, as if "the invisible orders of thrones, sovereignties, authorities, and powers" could exist apart from the Lord of history.

To correct these ascetic and ritualist extremists, Paul first located Christ not in the desert or among the rites, but in the middle of "all things" which he held together. So you have to put on the spectacles again "to see" the scope of divine creativity to which Paul points. The text is clear: "In him everything in heaven and on earth was created"; spatial stretches will never find models for all that Christ encompasses. That is the Christ in the *cosmos*.

Then, with a drastic leap, Paul moves secondly to the Christ in the congregation, among the sweaty, faltering, fallible people up close to us, the spouses and neighbors and fellow lay persons who so often provide such difficult tests when we must see Christ in them and be Christ to them.

And, thirdly, as Christ is "the head of the body, the church," Paul shows that God makes the individual "alive" in Christ. The people who sing about "The Lord of the Dance" have that clue right: So long as Christian faith implies that we must be passive and inert and timid, we have not caught the daring of his leap into our world.

What does this text from Paul . . . have to do with *your* creativity, in your immeasurably distant and diverse worlds? We find the answers when we follow the Christ of this text. He is not nature, but he leaves his trail in it; once more, let us stick faithfully to the text: His is the primacy over all created things. In him everything in heaven and on earth was created. The New Testament is full of words like "Behold!" "Look!" "See!" In the midst of the scenes of ashes, dust, silence, and death, this Christ is "the first to return from the dead," after his cross, the first mark of "the new creation." Can you ever look at the old creation in the old confining ways again?

After following his dwelling among us, his death, his "first birth" in the new creation, we revisit all the old scenes, remember how "all things" are created through him in art, music, writing; in politics among people, in professions where your decisions determine futures, in public service where human hands extend Christ's own, in a business world of temptation and opportunity. Here are the places where he comes.

Listen once more: "In him the complete being of God, by God's own choice, came to dwell." (Col. 1:19, NEB) The Christian Good News, the biblical promise, is that you will never again be alone in the midst of "all things." They will distract and confuse but never overwhelm you, once you see them "hold together" in him.

If he has power over everything "invisible" and "visible," the terror of the storm abates, however much as humans we . . . may be at its mercy. You will still live amid shock and devastation and the quaking and chaos of "earth," and will know that "visible" powers still can imprison the innocent—and are doing it this day. The "invisible" powers need no manipulation or scrutiny, after he came, and the most elaborate "thrones," as Paul calls them, though they dazzle, cannot enthrall you. "Dominions" live on, but their final power to enslave is gone; "principalities" are a threat, but you can sneer, and many Christians who carry crosses today do just that; "authorities" still knock on doors, but they cannot invade the recesses of the secure heart.

Tomorrow the chaos will still look like chaos, the alienation of our cities will remain visible, the plot of life will still be hard to piece together. But do you have the new eyes? Then you will see in the human junkyard of the old creation the scene where his order emerges in the order of human cities. Peter Berger has even had the audacity to say that New York is a "signal of transcendence." If he can find the sign there, then . . . all our other places will seem bursting with promise.

The immanent Christ carries the "beyond" and his "otherness" into our midst. "He is the origin of the church," "in all things supreme," whether in our large gatherings, where we come out of dispersal and hiding in the city to sign his presence; whether in the presence of the "many nations" and peoples and races in whom Paul delighted; among old and young, rich and poor, we all draw our life from him.

Paul uses the most vital and awesome images. You have no life apart from Christ the head; cut off from him nothing coheres or coordinates. But if he is the head of the body, our reflexes connect with his impulses. "The first to return from the dead," he was able to "reconcile the whole universe to himself." Our imaginations cannot encompass all of the "all things" that cohere in him—the catalogs and curricular, phone books and libraries are timid reminders. In the midst of all that world "he made peace through the shedding of his blood upon the Cross." There, abandoned by God, he brought us all into communion with him. We are reconciled.

On Sunday and the other six days of this week, what does it mean for us to be "creative" in the light of the Cross? Certainly we should be serene and confident, since the "powers" do not dominate. Just as certainly, we cannot abandon the world and its people to themselves and their problems. Each of you must find your creative sphere. Christ, the "immanent" Christ, is never directly seen in that world but always indirectly, through the sign of his Cross. Whether as the token of an ended day or the sign of one newly begun, with the spectacles and vision Paul provides, you will see your work in a new light because you will see him in new ways and places— if, that is, the Spirit has convinced you that in him *all things* hold together.

Conclusion

BEING
WITNESSES

And you shall be my witnesses . . ."—Christ's charge to his first followers and Christ's charge to us. In a comment on witnessing, George McDonald, the English cleric and novelist who so influenced C. S. Lewis, once said, "The time for speaking comes rarely. The time for being never departs."

These pages represent a lot of speaking; by me, on paper, and by those who spoke from the podium or in workshops at the Congress of the Laity. I hope before God that the congress and this book that comes out of it combine into one of those rare times when speaking is in order—speaking out of a conviction that God is calling the Christian laity of North America to unity, to intellectual and spiritual maturity, and to engagement in the world for God's glory and human welfare.

Our highest calling is to *be* witnesses—steadfast, caring, visionaries of hope in a world of shadows; to embody the light of Christ. Doing flows from being, for what we are, we do. Remembering the beam and the mote, George McDonald also said, "To try too hard to make people good is to make them worse: The only way to do good is to be good." Many of the tensions within the Christian family, it seems to me, arise from trying too hard to do—to reform structures, to convert the world, without first *being*. Advocates of personal evangelism and champions of social activism often try to justify what they do by casting aspersions on what the other side is doing—all of us trying too hard.

In my understanding, being witnesses means proclaiming the Gospel. Bearing in mind McDonald's warning against too much talk, it means the word of verbal testimony, wisely, appropriately, and timely spoken. Being witnesses also means, as Matthew 25 makes abundantly clear, feeding the hungry, welcoming the stranger, clothing the naked and caring for the sick and imprisoned, and exploring the contemporary ramifications of those mandates. It means prayer and worship—study, praise, thanksgiving, confession, dedication, and renewal through the sacraments. It means mutual love between husband and wife, parents and children; paying attention to people and their needs; receiving and giving forgiveness. Being witnesses means joy in winter's snow and the birds of spring; awe of mountain grandeur and bosomy surf. All such being leads to doing, but only as our particular individual and corporate activities emerge from what we are in obedience to Christ. None of us can judge how the being-doing mix, the personal-social paradox, is best expressed by others.

One thing the Christian laity of North America is: diverse. Its diversity is its essence and its glory in our Lord: one body, many members; one Spirit, many gifts; one vine, many branches. The diversity of the laity is its blessing—blessing in our many colors of skin and sounds of tongue; blessing in our cultural variety; blessing in our ecclesiastical and liturgical pluralism; and blessing in the richness of our individual histories, talents, and callings.

And as the family of faith is diverse, so are the forms of being witnesses along the edge where hope intersects despair in this world. Leslie Weatherhead told the story of a young nurse who was seeing a patient through his final illness. As the patient sinks lower and lower, the nurse goes to the doctor, a man of faith, to say, "Doctor, if he dies, I don't know what I'll say to his wife." The physician replies, "Don't say anything to his wife, just make her a cup of tea." Weatherhead's comment was that if wine poured out on the altar is the symbol of the uttermost love of God for humanity, then that tea was sacred, too, offered by a minister of God who happened to be wearing a nurse's uniform.

A minister of God in a nurse's uniform! Or the uniform of an executive or mechanic or ballerina, astronaut, farmer, sanitation worker, teacher, bank teller, journalist, lawyer, housewife or carpenter. That is our lay calling—to be ministers of and witnesses to the transcendent God in all the everyday uniforms of immanence; love spread wide in all its beautifully diffuse uniforms. The goal is Christlike mature character, in our individual lives, in the corporate body of the church, and in our Christian interaction with society.

Martin Marty told the joke of the elephant inside the block of marble—to get an elephant just chip away everything that does not look like an elephant. It is no joke that in each person, in our essence as human beings, is the image of the God of love. We sometimes must keep chipping away at all the hardness and meanness and self-centeredness that keeps us from recognizing the image of love in us. We are helped toward Christlikeness by many different chisels. Pain and despair can be chisels, and forgiveness and joy; there are Damascus-road experiences and emerging awareness, ordinary moments of anxiety or solitude, underserved graces and services we perform for others, and we die some as we are transformed into the living image of hope.

Hope is paradoxical, bending toward the "other world" of God's Kingdom and "this world" at the same time. And one of the mysteries of faith is that Christians formed in the image of hope can bend both ways at once without breaking. In Christ, "all things hold together." So, for the sake of the glory of God and for the sake of our brothers and sisters in this life, we can move far out onto the edge of hope, confident that Christ the center is also at all the edges.

But how do we know all things cohere in Christ? How do we know hope is stronger than despair? How do we know a church alive with all the energy of the lay potential is not a pipe dream? How do we know that truth and beauty will not fail, that discussions of transcendence and immanence are not merely fancy word games, that Christian unity is willed of God, that preoccupation with God gives social reform practical hope? How do we know love will not die?

We know only by faith. Troubled and doubting, wooed by despair, still we believe. "Lord, I believe. Help my unbelief."

When Jesus cried from the cross, "My God, my God, why have you forsaken me?" he experienced despair and doubt for us all and, at the same time, sealed the faithful with a hope that transforms our despairs. Hope comes from the Cross and, therefore, paradoxical hope is the only kind we have, for the cross is the paradox of death being prelude to life. This paradox, as G. K. Chesterton said, is not in God but in us, in our limited understanding, our unbalanced perception of truth, and our confused thinking. "The fault, dear Brutus, is . . . in ourselves that we are underlings."

Underlings? Yes, we are that, and finite and lacking in perfect knowledge and understanding of all mysteries; yet on the morning of the third day after the Cross on Golgotha, everything changed and in that empty tomb in a garden we, too, were resurrected to hope and faith and love. Our Lord is here and also goes before us, and when we acknowledge him, despair of this world or the next can have no grip on us. For Easter's dawn fully reveals what every sunrise says and what Jesus had known from the start: Hope always wins, even if it has to lose first.

AUTHORS AND
CONTRIBUTORS

HOWARD BUTT has long developed a wide variety of organizations and programs on family and church renewal through lay-theological-education and lay-ministry, including that of the Texas Hill Country retreat center Laity Lodge. He is Vice Chairman of the board of the H. E. Butt Grocery Company, board Chairman of Laity Lodge and Christian Men, Inc. (public charities related to the H. E. Butt Foundation) and a Southern Baptist layman. Author of *The Velvet Covered Brick* on Christian leadership, he was General Chairman of the North American Congress of the Laity.

PETER L. BERGER is professor of sociology at Rutgers University, New Brunswick, N.J., and associate editor of *Worldview*, the magazine of the Council on Religion and International Affairs. A Lutheran, born in Vienna, he is past president of the Society for the Scientific Study of Religion, and author of numerous books including *The Noise of Solemn Assemblies, A Rumor of Angels, Pyramids of Sacrifice*, and *Facing Up to Modernity*. His Ph.D. degree is from the New School of Social Research in New York City.

PETER F. DRUCKER, also born in Vienna, is a management consultant specializing in business and economic policy and, since 1971, Clarke Professor of Social Science and Management at the Claremont Graduate School in California. He taught at New York University for twenty-one years and has written fourteen books on political and economic themes including *The End of Economic Man, The Future of Industrial Man, Management for Results, The Age of Discontinuity,* and *Men, Ideas, and Politics.* A doctorate in law is from Frankfurt University, and his religious background is Calvinist.

GERALD R. FORD, the thirty-eighth president of the United States, and his wife, Betty, were honorary chairpersons of the North American Congress of the Laity. A twelve-term congressman from Michigan before becoming vice president in 1973, he is an attorney, a graduate of the University of Michigan and Yale University, and an Episcopalian.

EUGENE C. KENNEDY is professor of psychology at Loyola University, Chicago, and a principal figure in American pastoral counseling. The author of more than a hundred articles for Roman Catholic magazines, his twenty-six books include *On becoming A Counselor, Sexual Counseling, A Time for Being Human, The Return to Man, A Time for Love, The People Are the Church,* and *The New Sexuality: Myths, Fables and Hang-ups.* He received the Ph.D. degree from The University of Chicago.

THOMAS E. HOWARD is professor of English language and literature at Gordon College, Wenham, Massachusetts, and an international authority on C. S. Lewis, the late English writer. An Episcopalian, he holds the Ph.D. degree from New York University and has written widely for religious and general magazines. Among his books are *Christ the Tiger, An Antique Drum, Once Upon a Time . . . God,* and *Splendor in the Ordinary.*

FESTO KIVENGERE, bishop-in-exile of the Church of Uganda (Anglican), was a convenor of the International Congress on World Evangelization held in Lausanne, Switzerland, in 1974. Educated in Uganda, England, and the United States (Pittsburgh Theological Seminary), he is a leader of African Enterprise, an evangelistic ministry, and a member of the World Council of Churches' Commission on World Mission and Evangelism. His books include *When God Moves, Jesus, Our Reality, Love Unlimited,* and *I Love Idi Amin,* the latter a personal Christian response to the political dictator responsible for the bishop's flight from his country.

MARTIN E. MARTY is Fairfax M. Cone Distinguished Service Professor at the University of Chicago, where he teaches church history in the Divinity School, and is associate editor of *The Christian Century,* coeditor of *Church History,* and author of the newsletter *Context.* Winner of the National Book Award for *Righteous Empire: The Protestant Experience in America,* his numerous other books include *A Nation of Believers, Religion, Awakening and Revolution, The Fire We Can Light, Protestantism,* and *The Modern Schism.* He is an ordained Lutheran.

ABIGAIL MCCARTHY, novelist, autobiographer, and columnist, is a Roman Catholic lay leader and national figure in Church Women United, an ecumenical organization. A contributor to *Commonweal* magazine, her autobiography, *Private Faces / Public Places,* and her first novel, *Circles,* explore a world she knew as the wife of a United States senator. She is recipient of the Marymount Medal of Christian Excellence and the Trinity Medal for "bridge building."

MALCOLM MUGGERIDGE was educated at Selwyn College, Cambridge, before becoming a globe-trotting journalist for the Manchester *Guardian* and other British newspapers. Editor of *Punch,* celebrated wit and social critic, his career was expanded in the nineteen sixties with his conversion to Christianity. His books with religious themes include *Jesus Rediscovered, Something Beautiful for God, Jesus,* and *Paul: Envoy Extraordinary* (with Alec Vidler), which emerged from a British Broadcasting Corp. series on the Apostle.

JOHN P. NEWPORT is professor of philosophy and contemporary art at Rice University, Houston, Texas, having taught previously at Baylor University and several theological seminaries. He received the Ph.D. degree from the University of Edinburgh and a Th.D. from Southern Baptist Theological Seminary, Louisville, Kentucky. He is ordained Southern Baptist. Among his books are *Theology and Contemporary Art Forms; Demons, Demons; The Biblical and Occult Worlds,* and *Why Christians Fight over the Bible.*

ARMAND M. NICHOLI, II, M.D. is on the faculties of both the Harvard Medical School and Harvard College. Educated at Cornell University, the New York Medical College, and the University of Rochester and Harvard, he has been senior staff psychiatrist to students at Harvard and Radcliffe College. He was elected a fellow of the American Psychiatric Association in 1972, has published widely in medical and psychiatric journals, and is editor of the new and widely acclaimed *Harvard Guidebook to Modern Psychiatry.* He is Congregationalist.

THOMAS M. REAVLEY is professor at the University of Texas Law School, after having spent ten years as a justice on the Texas Supreme Court. A United Methodist educated at the University of Texas and Harvard University, he was Texas secretary of state in 1955–1957 and was associated with various law firms before being named a district judge in 1964. He is chancellor of the Southwest Texas Conference of his denomination.

JAMES RESTON has twice won the Pulitzer Prize in Journalism. Columnist and member of the board of directors of the *New York Times,* a graduate of the University of Illinois, and owner and copublisher with his wife of the *Vineyard Gazette* (on Martha's Vineyard). He was born in Scotland and is of Presbyterian origins. He has been decorated by the French Legion of Honor and the Order of St. Olaf in Norway, and is the author of three books, *Prelude to Victory, The Artillery of the Press,* and *Sketches in the Sand.*

ELLIOTT WRIGHT, a free-lance writer, was formerly an editor and reporter for Religious News Service. A United Methodist, he holds master and doctoral degrees from the Vanderbilt University Divinity School, and has written for a wide variety of newspapers and magazines. His books include *Go Free, The Big Little School* (with Robert Lynn), and *Can These Bones Live? The Failure of Church Renewal* (with Robert Lecky). He is consultant to several national religious organizations.